Wiser & Better!

The Self Coaching Workbook For A Vibrant Life After 50

Greg Jordan

Workbook Owner_______________________

Contents

Introduction

Why You Need This Workbook

As the saying goes, "You're not getting older, you're getting wiser". Substitute "better" for "wiser", and you have two of the most quoted lines about getting older. You'll hear them used as a little lame gallows humor on any birthday after age 30. For some people, both statements are true. For others, neither seems close to being true.

This workbook helps people live up to both of those statements. It's for anyone who wants to experience more enjoyment and meaning as the unstoppable clock of life ticks away. The time to work on having a great latter stage of life is not after we realize we're old, but well before, while still youthful in thought.

Even a little preparation for the mid-life to latter years is well worth doing. Why? Because for people at or approaching their latter years, 21st century life presents choices that no generation before us has had, and we need to think about how to handle those choices.

Life after 50 can be more fulfilling than many of us have imagined. We have the opportunity to grow our place in the world – one characterized by joy and meaning - like no other time in history.

It would be a fair question if you were to ask yourself why should you use this workbook or listen to me on this topic? Let me explain.

In 2007, I was a consultant for a project called *Navigating Your Retirement,* which later morphed into *My Plan After 50.* The originator of that program was an EAP (Employee Assistance Program) provider in Des Moines, Iowa. They had the good vision to see that people who were approaching the retirement stage of their life often needed coaching to successfully handle the transition. Their clients in that stage of their career greatly benefitted from this project.

Sometime later, when they no longer wanted to pursue that line of coaching, the project was dropped. Knowing the value that the content provided to all manner of people who needed these additional skills, I contacted them and asked their permission to modify and publish some of these materials.

I'm grateful to them that they graciously agreed and as a result, you're holding **Wiser & Better**! in your hands.

Most recently, I've provided marketing services to a client in the senior care business for a few years now, and that's given me deeper insight into some of the universal issues related to managing the process of aging.

I've also been inspired by countless older people who are doing wonderful things every day in a world that overly values youth. And one personal example - the story of my own feisty Aunt Nancy has always inspired me.

Aunt Nancy is no longer with us, but as a young man I watched with amazement as she, a childhood polio survivor who never had use of her left arm, refused to let her disability interfere with her life in any way. It didn't stop her from graduating from art school before I was born, nor did it stop her from creating lots of her own oil paintings.

Until well into her 80's she would board a bus by herself and head into Washington DC to the National Gallery of Art, just to see an exhibit by a favorite artist. She was an independent, nonstop-living woman who wasn't about to let her age or physical limitations get the best of her.

My personal life experiences have picked up where my aunt left off. I'm still active in business in my early 70's, I competed in my first triathlon at age 59, earned a black belt in Aikido at age 62, and I practice a daily physical exercise routine.

I became a late life meditation and Reiki practitioner, and I jumped headfirst into the digital world, becoming a Google-certified digital advertising marketer at age 65. I'm blessed with an appetite for learning and trying new things.

I'm convinced that all of these experiences, combined with a positive mental attitude helped me to navigate through my own personal calamities. The power of a resilient attitude that moves us forward when things aren't ideal is available to all of us – even, or perhaps especially - as we get older.

What's Ahead In This Workbook

I'll readily admit that none of my previous experience makes me an expert on aging, nor is this workbook the last word on living a vibrant life after 50. You'll need to discover all answers for yourself. ***Wiser & Better****!* provides a model, perspective, and tools – a roadmap to assist you in answering those questions for yourself.

A lot about the world has changed since the *My Plan After 50,* project, and although still a major event for many people, retirement isn't an option for a growing number of Americans. But the ability to make the most of life is within us all, retired or not.

The essential question is: **What can we do to prepare for living a vital life long after we've lost our 30's 40's and 50's to the passage of time?**

I've taken some of the tools of *My Plan After 50,* updated and added to them, and most importantly, shifted the focus from retirement to mastering life skills no matter what your job or financial situation is. This workbook is part inspiration, part mentor, part journal, part idea generator, and hopefully all helpful to you.

As we reach the midpoint in our lives, we may find ourselves seeking a new sense of direction, wondering: "What's life all about, really? What have I accomplished? What do I want to do with the next phase of my life?"

Whether you're considering retirement, or don't see it in the near future, what's in this workbook are things you can do NOW to shape your life path … **and develop the life skills necessary to make the years ahead the BEST phase of our lives!**

In *The Virtues of Aging*, former President Jimmy Carter describes an interview with Barbara Walters. After having reviewed the many stages of Carter's life from the farm in Plains, Georgia, to military duty, to business, to the Governor's Mansion, to the Presidential Mansion and back to Plains, she asked him to name the best years of his life? He immediately and heartily responded: "NOW. These are the best years."

Why do you think that is? What do you think Jimmy Carter knows, does or has, that gives him that enviable reality? I believe that he has learned and can apply essential skills for successful aging. He knows that the ideal life path is one on which we learn from each and every experience and phase of our lives - gather the good stuff, and discard whatever is not useful to us. We develop essential life skills; we keep, and spend time with, the friends that are true; we play in ways that are healthful and that we enjoy.

Many people think adequate financial planning will assure a good later phase of life and perhaps eventual retirement. What I've found is that financial planning is essential, but **a successful life after 50 is much more than a matter of financing your nest egg.** It requires attention to and development of other important areas of one's life. I call these areas *the 8 Wiser & Better! elements.*

On average, people can look to 25 or more years of life after 50. We know that this generation has varied interests and a great desire to contribute to society while having fun. Will this phase of your life be marked by both opportunities and difficulties? Most assuredly!

Will we be beset by the problems of boredom or depression that we have seen in many of the former generations as they aged? Of course!

But there's good news. **Through the assessments and learning processes laid out in this workbook, you can identify areas of personal growth and potential difficulties, and take steps *now* to maximize the positive and minimize the negative impact on your years after 50 and beyond.**

One word of caution. I can guarantee that you will not find all the answers, or a problem free future within these pages. **But it will help you think through and control some of the challenges that come with aging, and contribute to the enjoyment of life**. It's intended to start you on a path of inquiry, discovery, and actions that will increase the probability of getting what you want out of your future.

I encourage you to jump in, do the work use *Wiser & Better!* as a guide to stimulate ideas and thinking. **Tackle the deceptively simple questions and exercises in a thoughtful, lighthearted way, engage others in discussion, and self-direct yourself to a better life ahead**. After all, it is a *work*book.

How To Use This Workbook

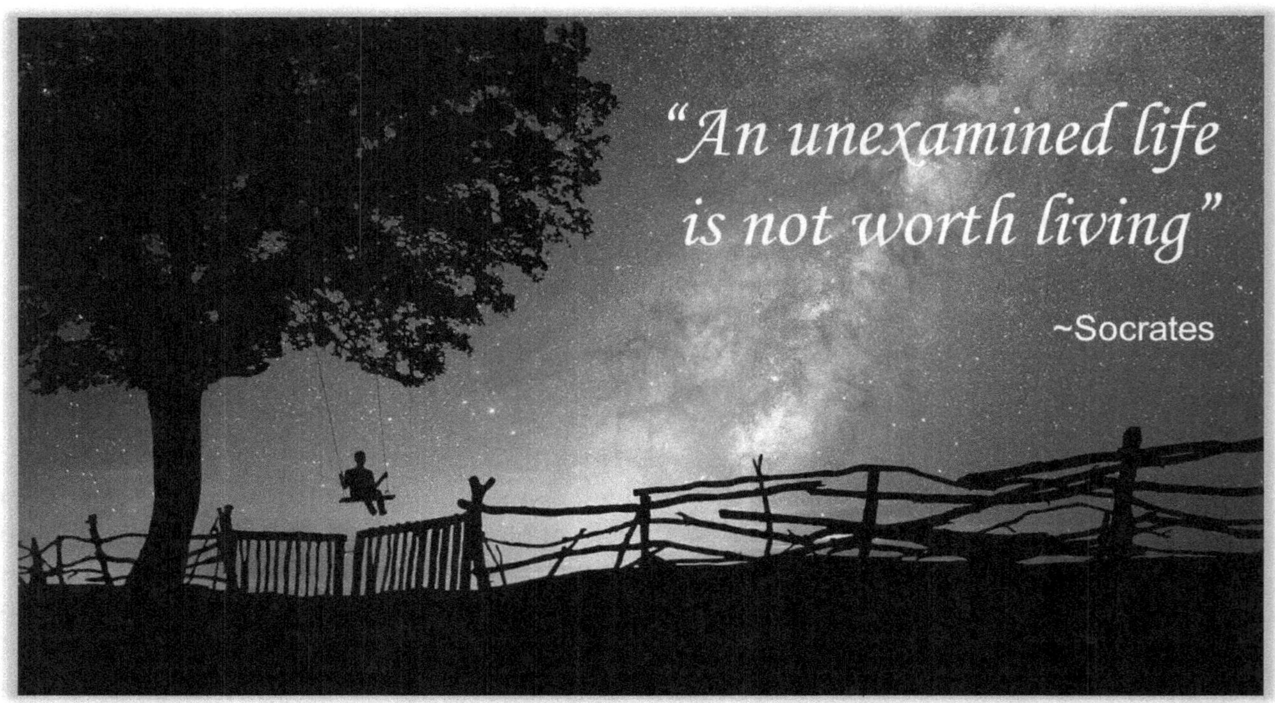

There are very few rules to use this workbook. It's flexible so you can work on what's most important in your life. You're in total control of how you use it.

Make it your own. To make any progress, **you'll need to do the exercises and write down your personal notes and actions.**

It's well known that the handwriting process connects to your brain in meaningful ways. Along with the more structured questionnaires and checklists, I included plenty of blank pages and spaces for you to use in any way that's helpful. **Make them messy with written thoughts notes, drawings or pasted images** (you don't have to have any art skills – just the intent to create something memorable).

Blank pages, margins, and text boxes are useful guidelines, yet there's no need to write between the lines. The more you write, draw, doodle, create notes, and document your personal insights, the more it will become a useful personal tool in making changes in your life.

Pick the most important elements to work on in any order and at any time. It's up to you to decide which of these are most important or most interesting. Revisit each element from time to time, and create additional ideas, goals, and actions. Why? Because elements that are least important to you now may become more important as circumstances inevitably change.

You'll get better results when you discuss your insights with trusted people. The assessments, goal setting and journaling are individual thinking exercises. You'll find that after you've completed them, you'll be in the perfect frame of mind to discuss them with other people in your life. Almost certainly, additional richness and clarity will emerge if you decide to do this.

Finally, have fun with it. These topics can be weighty and serious. But approach them all with a lightness of attitude, knowing that the thought and work you put into each element can refresh your outlook and add fun and enjoyment to your future. Just decide to make it a fun and rewarding exercise.

The workbook is organized into Idea and Concept Blocks, Thinking Blocks and Action Blocks.

Idea and Concept Blocks are indicated by this symbol of the lit lightbulb icon. They contain thoughts, ideas and explanations to help you think about each element. It can't possibly answer all the questions you might have but can identify some new ideas for you to explore.

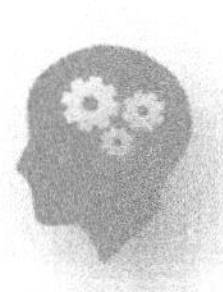

The **Thinking Blocks** - indicated by the thinking head icon - help you to think about where you are now. They're self-assessments – simple questions that can be profoundly useful in designing your future. Almost without exception, some new thoughts or ideas will occur to you, just by taking the assessments. Keep in mind that these are not comprehensive assessments, they're tools to get you to think about major factors that influence your life after 50.

The primary benefits of taking these assessments are that you'll be able to more easily recognize gaps and opportunities for self-improvement, and set more accurate goals for yourself - goals that will stretch, but not exceed your capabilities.

The **Action Blocks**, indicated by the task manager icon, are where you'll get to identify goals, and things to do in order to approach your latter years with the most success.

Journal pages are included to let any revelations, ideas or actions flow from your mind and pen. Write anywhere you please – take notes, draw, and make it your own. Capture important thoughts and keep moving through to other sections.

You'll get the most benefit when you thoroughly engage with this process and revisit it from time to time. Most of all, enjoy this exploration, and we hope it stimulates thinking and actions that lead you to a vibrant life after 50, 60, and beyond.

The 8 *Wiser & Better!* Elements

	Maximizing Health and Wellness
	Handling Job and Career Options
	Adapting to Life's Changes
	Managing Family Relationships
	Building a Network
	Living a Meaningful Life
	Ensuring a Balanced Life
	Working Your Finances

Thinking Block - Attitudes about Aging

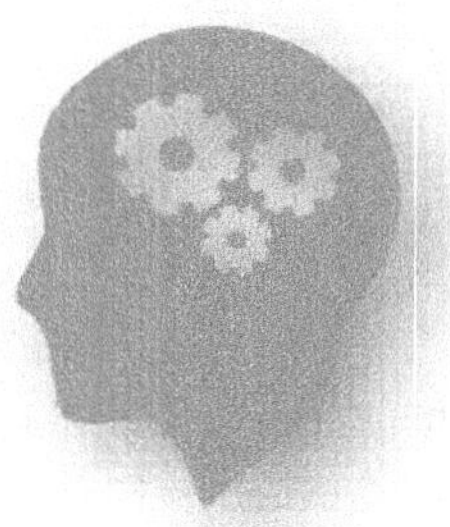

Before you get started with the elements of **Wiser & Better!** we want you to get into your first thinking block right away. Your attitudes about aging will influence everything that comes after this. So, it's important to grapple with this one at as deep a level as you can.

Our attitudes towards aging (and the setting of positive intentions) significantly affect our health as we grow older. Researchers at Yale University suggest that looking forward to growing older could actually help you to live longer. Results of the 23-year-long study of people aged 50 and over revealed that those who had a positive attitude towards aging lived roughly seven and a half years longer than participants who were dreading reaching their twilight years.

Further, brain research tells us that your brain is like a super-computer, and what we tell ourselves in thought and belief is like the operating system that runs that computer and influences everything we do. Our attitudes are part of that operating system. They're comprised of beliefs and values that define how we view the world and our own lives. Attitudes influence our feelings, expectations and behaviors. **By becoming aware of our attitudes, we can challenge the underlying beliefs and values, as well as alter how we choose to feel and behave.**

This is a brief inventory of personal attitudes towards aging. Review the paired statements and choose the number that best represents your attitude. Review your responses in the center column of this assessment.

Attitudes about Aging - Assessment		
I anticipate my life after 60 to be very exciting.	5　4　3　2　1	Compared to previous stages, life after 60 will be slow and dull.

I see older people as vibrant and alive.	5 4 3 2 1	I see older people as on a gradual but persistent slide towards death.
I embrace the physical changes I am experiencing.	5 4 3 2 1	I feel cheated by my body.
I expect that I will be involved in lots of things the older I get.	5 4 3 2 1	I am expecting my world to become narrower as I age.
Older people have many advantages over younger people.	5 4 3 2 1	Older people are disadvantaged compared to younger people.
The second half of my life will be the best half of my life.	5 4 3 2 1	I know that my best years are in my past.
As I become older, I will take more (non-financial) risks.	5 4 3 2 1	As I become older, I need to take fewer (non-financial) risks.
Older individuals have a great deal to give to society.	5 4 3 2 1	Older people are worn and tired, and have little left to give.
I may not run as fast, but I still can have a good physical life.	5 4 3 2 1	I'm broken down and getting worse. Why fight it?

In the space that follows, write down any of the attitudes reflected in paired statements for which you selected a 1, 2 or 3.

Consider if these are the kind of scores that will help you to have a strong, successful life after 50.

As you reflect on your life, including your upbringing, what underlying values and/or beliefs may be influencing your attitudes about aging?

If you believe you have the ability to challenge and change your attitudes about aging, what will you do to address those attitudes that may concern you about how you face and live out your own aging process? Use the action block below.

Note: Remember that attitudes are habits of thought. To change an attitude, it's first necessary to change the way you think. This may not be a quick process – because it's a habit. Your attitudes can be changed by consistent language you use with yourself, internally, and with others. Try reading more on these topics or seek out other thoughts and ideas that relate.

I will take the following actions regarding my present attitudes about aging:

Maximizing Health and Wellness

Wellness is multi-faceted and includes our bodies, minds, emotions, and that elusive but all-encompassing spiritual part

---

The years after 50 can be the longest and most fulfilling of life's stages. This requires taking care of your overall health through practices that enhance all the areas of physical, mental, emotional and spiritual wellness, any of which can easily be neglected in our busy world.

Physical	Mental
Spiritual	Emotional

People all over the world have used this matrix as a simple model of a health and wellness for thousands of years. Here's how each one of these four aspects of health relate to a successful and joyful life after 50.

Physical exercise, and new medical diagnostic and treatment tools prolong the length and quality of our lifespan far beyond any other generation's.
Mental health using educational and behavioral tools make life more interesting and enjoyable.
Emotional support from those in our family and social network help us manage life's twists and turns.
Developing spirituality helps us see and connect to our fundamental beliefs and the deeper elements of our nature.

Again, attitude is a most important part of health. Three of the most positive attitudes that impact your health are resilience (one of the 8 *Wiser and Better!* elements covered later), gratitude (see the Gratitude section under "Living a Balanced Life", and abundance. There have been many studies that show their connection with reduced stress and health.

As Dr. Andrew Weil, the noted health expert, says: "I hardly notice my aging on a day-to-day basis. When I look in the mirror in the morning, [I] seem the same as the day before. But . . . looking at old photographs, I can't help but notice the physical change that has taken place . . ."

Preparing for a healthy life after 50 will include attention to our long-term health and wellness. Such factors as diet, exercise, use of alcohol, tobacco, prescription drugs, vitamins and other food supplements, all require attention. They can all be important contributors to your longevity and to the quality of your life, whether retired or not.

Health and wellness at this age isn't characterized by clinging to a denial of aging, but learning to adapt to that reality and, as Dr. Weil asserts, "to be in the best health we can at any age."

Thinking Block – Health and Wellness

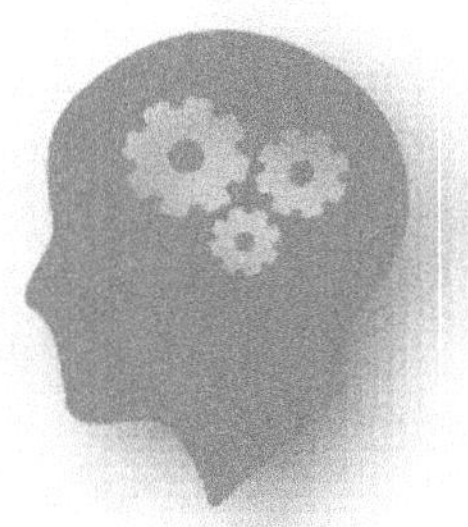

1 *Take this assessment and check the column to indicate if it's a Strength or Weakness area, or if it doesn't matter right now (N – neutral). Do not overthink this. The purpose is to get you looking for areas to build on, and areas to improve in.*

Assessment - Maximizing Your Health and Wellness	S	N	W
Physical			
Good physical health is important to me			
My personal habits are conducive to good health			
I've had a physical exam within the last year			
I plan for and get good rest and relaxation			
I have a regular exercise program			
I minimize the amount of processed foods and sugars in my diet			
My weight is under control			
I don't get sick or miss work often because of illness			
I know the danger signs of major diseases like stroke, cancer, etc.			
I understand my private health care plan and its options			
I understand Medicare Benefit Options			
I know what my average blood pressure and heart rate is			
I emphasize good health with my family			
Mental			
I make practical, common sense decisions			
I focus the majority of my time on the most important 20% of my challenges			
I anticipate problems and opportunities			
I have sound problem-solving abilities			
I'm organized and efficient about the practical aspects of my life			
I set priorities for spending my time			

I continuously learn and develop myself			
I know my personal strengths and weaknesses			
I don't hesitate to adopt technologies or new methods to improve my life			
Emotional & Spiritual			
I understand and manage my internal emotions			
I get upset frequently at other people's actions			
I often speak angrily to people in my life and regret it later			
I practice gratitude in my everyday life			
I spend time regularly in prayer, quiet thought or meditation			
I keep a positive attitude about life			
I find myself frequently in win/lose arguments			
I use sound problem-solving skills to help manage my emotions			
I am comfortable with my own spiritual beliefs and practices			
Other people do not define my happiness			
I understand and manage the stress levels in my personal and work life			

Work On It

Now, with your strength and weakness areas in mind, list the most important ones and jot down your thoughts on how your strengths will help, and your weaknesses will hurt you in your life after 50.

My Main Strengths	How This Will Help

My Main Weaknesses	How This Could Be A Problem

3 *Using the table that follows, write down a goal, a motivating statement, specific actions to deliver that goal, and a date that you would like to complete it by. This will be your plan for making changes in your health and wellness that will serve you well as the years go by. Consider creating goals based on your strengths and opportunities, and in areas such as:*

- *Nutrition and diet*
- *Exercise and weight control*
- *Flexibility*
- *Use of tobacco and alcohol*
- *Mental and learning*
- *Emotional management*
- *Spirituality*
- *Health management*
- *Health Insurance*

- *Write as specifically as you can your desired behavior change (goal). You may want to use the SMART goal methodology for this (Specific, Measurable, Achievable, Realistic and Timely). For example, a SMART goal would be: "Explore Medicare options with an expert and choose a plan by October 1 of this year". You may want to identify more than one desired change.*

- *Write a motivation statement (affirmation) that you can return to as a reminder of why that behavior change is important to you.*

- *Make a note of what resources you'll need in order to successfully implement and sustain your desired change. Keep in mind what you have learned from previous efforts, so that you can anticipate and overcome barriers.*
- *Finally, identify a reward that you'll give yourself when you have attained your desired change.*

Goals	Affirmation	Action I Will Take	By When

Goals	Affirmation	Action I Will Take	By When

 Congratulations! You've wrestled with some significant questions and have the beginnings of a plan to help you create a vibrant life after 50 in the Health and Wellness element. It's a good stopping point with this element for now. Your next task is to take the actions that you promised yourself. Truthfully, your work here is only just beginning. Revisit this section as you need, and evaluate how you're doing against your goals.

It's a great time to discuss your goals, plans and learnings with a friend, spouse, coworker or someone else that you trust. Here are journal pages where you can write about anything that comes to mind regarding this topic. We'll see you in the next section!

Handling Job and Career Options

Work provides us with much more than a paycheck.

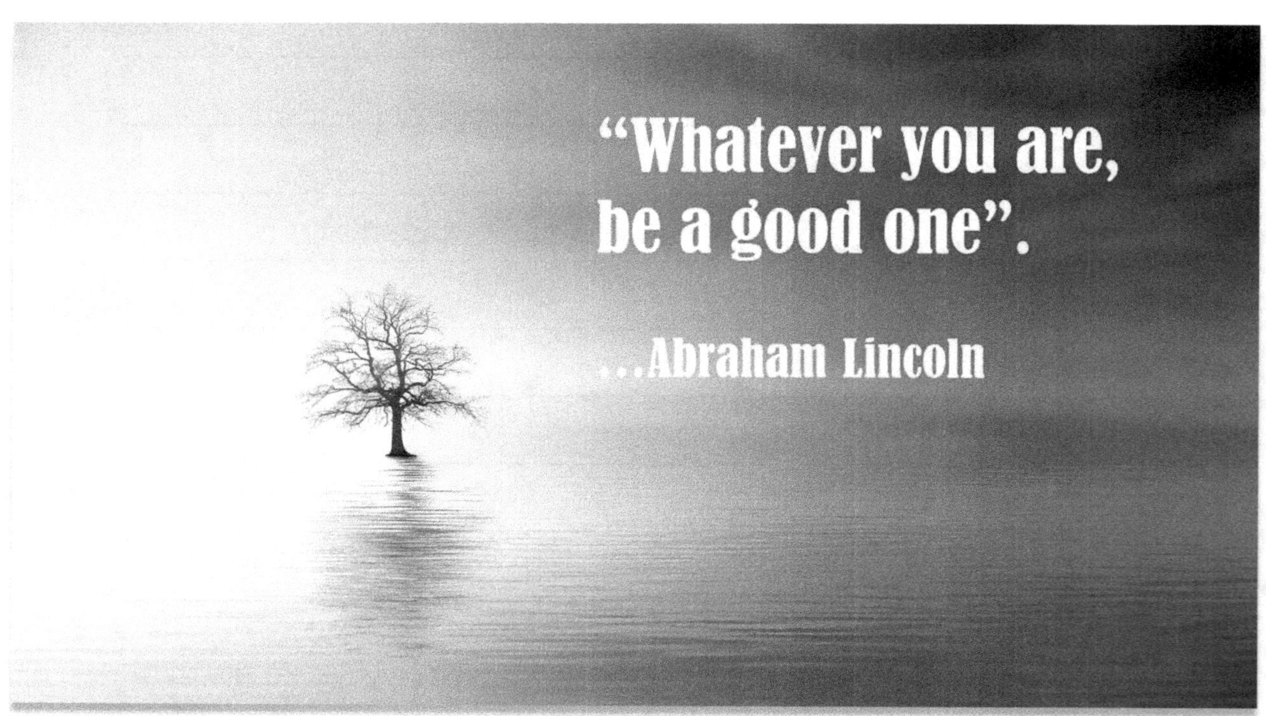

In this section, we examine the role of work in our daily lives, consider retirement and make adjustments based on our discoveries.

Most of us discover that this section leads us to numerous work-related options during this phase of life. Some will want to retire, some will need full-time income, others will start their own business; still others will work for the sheer joy of contributing their hard-earned experiences to better the world.

For those of you who want or need to work, what skills and characteristics do you have (or can develop) that will appeal to an employer? Just as importantly, ask yourself the question: "How can I live my passion through work that is meaningful and rewarding?"

During our career-building years, work provides us with much more than a paycheck. It brings a sense of order and predictability to our lives and provides a time management structure that affects much of our life. Work gives us purpose, meaning and identity. Successful life after 50 means finding ways to continue to receive all of these benefits, regardless of what career, work or retirement choice we make.

The constant increase in the cost of living has made it difficult for many to retire. Some surveys show that as much as 75% of the working Boomer population indicate that they don't think they'll ever retire, in the traditional sense of the word. **<u>How will you prepare for your future work life or retirement?</u>**

The urge and quest for meaningful activity at this stage of life is a natural, age-appropriate re-assessment. **Re-examining our work life at this stage is a good thing and can make all the difference in setting up our coming years to be the ones we can deeply enjoy!** It's at this time when what one author terms the "Crisis of Relevance" looms much more important to many of us than in our younger years…and there are biological and developmental reasons for that. In fact, research has clarified many of those reasons and that information is available and useful as we make the choices that work for us.

A few good examples of that are:
- The adult brain, contrary to previous beliefs, actually regenerates! That's right – we actually can grow new neurons and neuronal capabilities in later life, IF we use our brains in ways that promote such growth. How do you want to use your work hours in this phase of your life?
- As Dr. Gene Cohen points out in *The Mature Mind*, "The increasing use of both sides of the brain (in later adulthood) … can support a more balanced perspective on life that draws on both our logical, analytical powers and nonverbal, intuitive capacities." He explains that it is only when we are older that we have the capability of such "developmental intelligence." What are the unique skills and assets that you want to develop and utilize during those work hours?

It's s a sad fact that ageism is an operating dynamic in our workforce. It is sometimes very difficult for skilled, knowledgeable, experienced, and dedicated people in their 50's and 60's who want to work, to get a job, despite the great value they could bring.

In these situations, an option is for some people is to start their own business. Bloomberg.com recently reported the following: *"Starting a business during the traditional retirement years is rising: 55 to 64-year-olds accounted for 26% of new entrepreneurs in 2017, up from 15% in 1996.*

The reasons for this trend are many, but primarily, online skills and tools make it easier to start a business. In addition, as we pointed out earlier, retirement is not an option for many people, and **what better way to create an income then by leveraging in-demand skills and experiences that took years to build?**

Anticipating this situation, it's always wise to keep developing new skills that are valued in the workforce, and to online audiences. There are many entrepreneurial options available such as consulting, and online ecommerce opportunities.

Keep an up to date resume always available and building a network on social media network LinkedIn is a strategic asset for identifying people and opportunities, and displaying your skills and experiences to a broad business audience.

We have the chance to live our passion, and this workbook can help you find your passion and manifest it in the world, for the benefit of yourself and others. Your choices in the area of work are one of the *Wiser & Better!* elements essential to creating and maintaining a VIBRANT life after 50.

Thinking Block – Job and Career Options

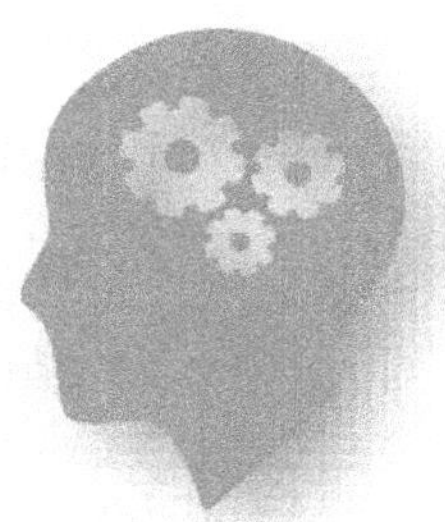

For each benefit, rate the degree to which work is a source of fulfillment for you, in the context of your life, with "5" meaning work that is your primary source of fulfillment and "1" meaning that work provides little or no fulfillment. For example, a person for whom co-workers comprise the majority of her after-work social group might well rate the first benefit a "5," while someone with a broad social network outside of work may rate the benefit a "1" or "2."

Do not overthink this. The purpose is to get you looking for areas to build on, and areas to improve in.

Assessment – Job and Career Options	1	2	3	4	5
Social and daily interaction with others					
Pays the bills					
Sense of knowing I make a difference					
A daily schedule and routine					
Having an identity, status, or place in society					
I'm happy being employed and doing what I do					
I have special skills from my current work that are in demand in the workplace					
My job or career allows me to further develop as a person or professional					
I know where I want to be with my job or career in 1 year					
I know where I want to be with my job or career in 10 years					
I have clear ideas and goals related to my retirement					

Work On It

The Place of Work in My Future

What about you? This exercise will ask you to engage in imaginative forward thinking. After all, much will occur over the next five to twenty years of your life, only some of which you'll be able to control. Even the most diehard, "I'll *never* retire" people will do well to give thought and planning to forced changes (e.g., a significant health incident or a business merger or acquisition) in their relationship to work.

Looking ahead over the next 20 years, how do you see your relationship with the world of work changing? Check the type of working arrangement you would like – 5, 10, 15 and 20 years for now.

Relationship to Work	5 years	10 years	15 Years	20 Years
Full-time work in the same field as today	☐	☐	☐	☐
Full-time work in a different field	☐	☐	☐	☐
Half-time or part-time work	☐	☐	☐	☐
Self-employment or start a business	☐	☐	☐	☐
Consultant	☐	☐	☐	☐
Volunteer work only	☐	☐	☐	☐
Some mix of volunteer and paid work	☐	☐	☐	☐
Retire	☐	☐	☐	☐
Other:	☐	☐	☐	☐

In completing this grid, what surprised you?

What changes need to occur for you to accomplish the working arrangements you checked?

What questions or concerns arose as you completed the grid?

As you move through any work transitions over the next 20 years, you'll want to ensure that you anticipate and address the impact on the benefits you currently derive from work. Take a few moments to review your Benefits of Work exercise and summarize them in the space below.

Replacing The Benefits From Work:

Go back and review your self-assessment for this section and you'll see that the left-hand column represents the benefits from working. Fill out the following table to form ideas on how you'll replace those benefits as you get older, or retire, or your job situation otherwise changes.

Benefits of Work	How Would I Replace It?

 *Using the table that follows, write down a goal, a motivating statement, specific actions to deliver that goal, and a date that you would like to complete it by. This will be your plan for making changes in your job and*

career situation that will serve you well as the years go by. Consider creating goals based on your strengths and opportunities, and in areas such as:

> *Developing new job skills such as computer or tech skills*
> *Replacing work benefits*
> *Income generating alternatives*
> *Career planning*
> *Retirement planning*

Write as specifically as you can your desired behavior change (goal). You may want to use the SMART goal methodology for this (Specific, Measurable, Achievable, Realistic and Timely). For example, a SMART goal would be: "Start a women's clothing design business by March of 2021". You may want to identify more than one desired change.
Write a motivation statement (affirmation) that you can return to as a reminder of why that behavior change is important to you.

Make a note of what resources you'll need in order to successfully implement and sustain your desired change. Keep in mind what you have learned from previous efforts, so that you can anticipate and overcome barriers.
Finally, identify a reward that you'll give yourself when you have attained your desired change.

Goals	Affirmation	Action I Will Take	By When

Goals	Affirmation	Action I Will Take	By When

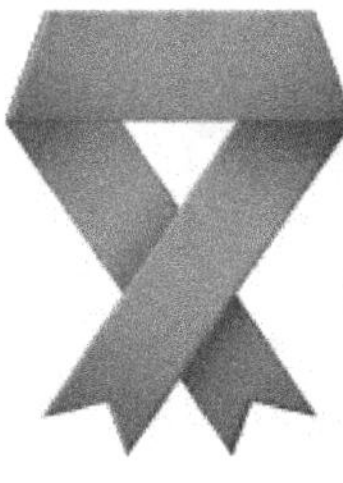

Congratulations! You've wrestled with some significant questions and have the beginnings of a plan to help you create a vibrant life after 50 in the job and career element. It's a good stopping point with this element for now. Your next task is to take the actions that you promised yourself. Truthfully, your work here is only just beginning. Revisit this section as you need, and evaluate how you're doing against your goals.

It's a great time to discuss your goals, plans, and learnings with a friend, spouse, coworker, or someone else that you trust. Below are journal pages where you can write or draw about anything that comes to mind regarding this topic. We'll see you in the next section!

Adapting to Life Changes - Resiliency

The ability to manage the ever-present changes in our lives and learn from mistakes and challenges is a vital skill that contributes to a vibrant life.

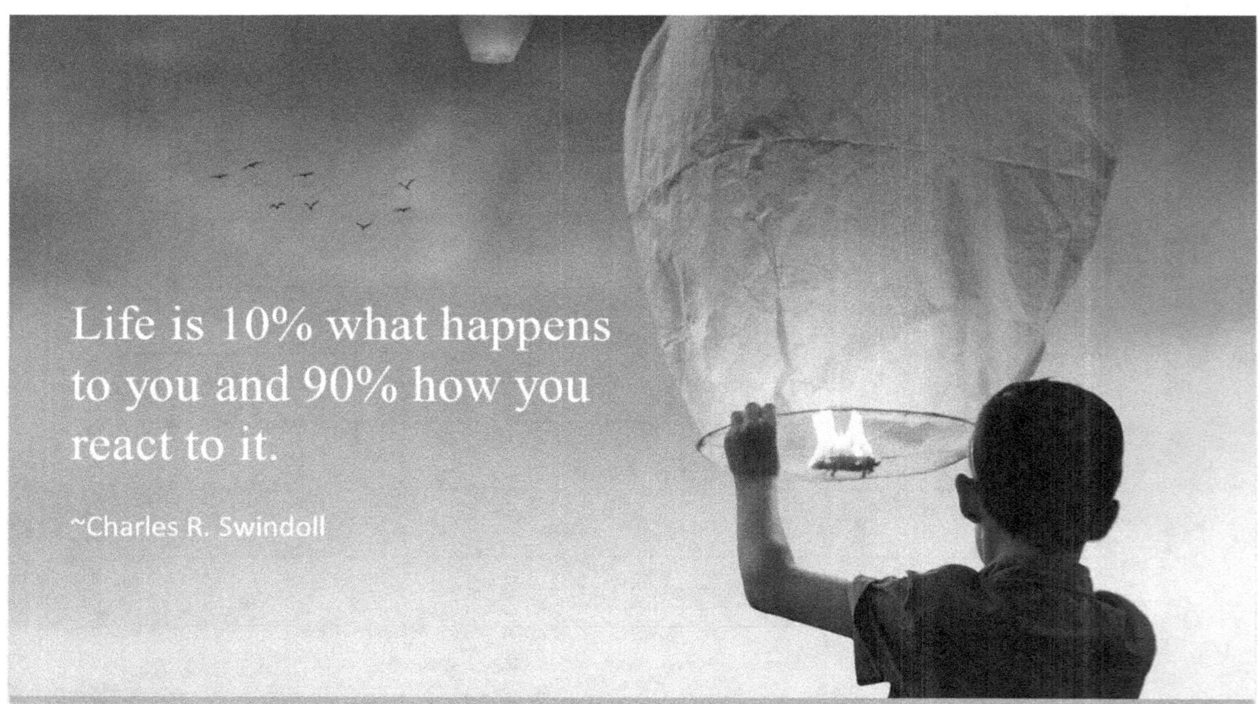

Merriam-Webster defines "resilience" as "an ability to recover from or adjust easily to misfortune or change." A counselor colleague of ours describes it as "the ability to turn trash into fuel." However you define it, the important question is: How resilient are you?

Do you feel generally optimistic, hopeful and confident when difficulties arise? Do you tend to adapt easily to change? Would you describe yourself as fairly flexible and OK with life's ambiguities? Do you customarily find the silver lining in problem situations, and do you have a good sense of humor? These are characteristics of resilient people and hallmarks of those who, as the Navajo say, know how to walk the "Beauty Path."

Resilient people cope better with the dynamics of living that are fundamental to the challenges of life after 50, such as the effects of aging on our bodies, and the loss of loved ones and friends. Simply put: by becoming more resilient, you'll improve your chances of a longer, healthier and higher quality of life!

Some people are naturally, highly resilient. Most of us, however, must hone this skill through intentional practice.   As with any positive skill development, increasing resilience takes understanding, commitment and effort. In his excellent book, *The Resilient Advantage*, Dr. Al Siebert postulates these steps for developing resiliency skills:

- Optimize your health and well-being.

- Develop good problem-solving skills.

- Develop inner gatekeepers (self-messages that speak on our behalf).

- Discover your talent for serendipity.

- Develop high-level resiliency.

Many research studies have made it clear that highly resilient people share the attribute of feeling personally responsible for how their lives go, and believe they have some control over events and their responses to them.

In fact, if you approach life's challenges with a focus on solving the problem (as opposed to reacting emotionally and disengaging), this ability will ripple out into other areas of your life – work success, personal relationships, individual health – in a remarkable way.

In this section you'll identify your resiliency status and have the opportunity to target, clearly and specifically, the aspects of resiliency that you wish to strengthen. Any skill development starts with intention – the decision to take action. I assure you; it is an exciting process! You'll discover that the effort you invest in enhancing your resilience as you move beyond 50 will reward you with strengths and abilities for living that you didn't know were possible!

Thinking Block – Resiliency

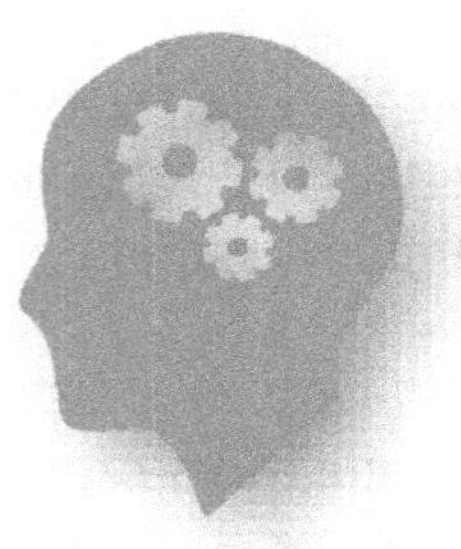

Rate Your Resilience!

For each of the following, give yourself the appropriate "score" (1 = This is not me at all; 2 = This is seldom me; 3 = Neutral; 4 = This is me fairly often; 5 = This is me!).

Do not overthink this. The purpose is to get you looking for areas to build on, and areas to improve in.

Assessment - Resiliency	
When I make mistakes, I look for lessons learned rather than blame myself.	
When life is chaotic, I focus, remain calm and take action to move forward.	
When change occurs that I have not initiated, I rapidly embrace or adapt to it.	
I tolerate high levels of uncertainty.	
I look on the bright side and expect things to turn out well.	
I am flexible and can make course corrections when someone or something alters my plans.	
I have a good sense of humor, can find humor in difficult situations and can laugh at myself.	
When I am experiencing difficulties, I can express my feelings to friends and family.	
I ask for help when I am anxious.	
When "bad" things happen, I seek the opportunities hidden there.	
I usually find the best in others and feel comfortable with people different from me.	
I like myself and feel confident.	
My friends, family and associates say I am a good listener.	

When given a project, I am good at figuring out what is the best way to proceed.	
I like to solve problems, and can balance creativity with practicality.	
I am usually flexible, depending on the demands of the situation.	
I am aware of my surroundings and the people with whom I interact.	
I am a learner and ask many questions.	
I can be very independent when appropriate, and I can also be cooperative.	
When I experience turbulence in my life, I adapt quickly.	
TOTAL SCORE (add the scores from each of the preceding statements)	

Here's how to interpret your scores:

Low

If you rated yourself at a 50 or less, you are probably struggling every day. Pressure usually gets the best of you. Even if someone is giving you a compliment, you may hear a hidden criticism. You see things as out of your control and often feel helpless. You are often self-critical and fearful.

Medium

Your score of 51-70 indicates that your resiliency skills are adequate for you to get by, but you can easily get stuck and not move forward. You may want others to tell you that you are OK more often than they're motivated to do so. You feel bumped around by life more than you feel in control of your situation.

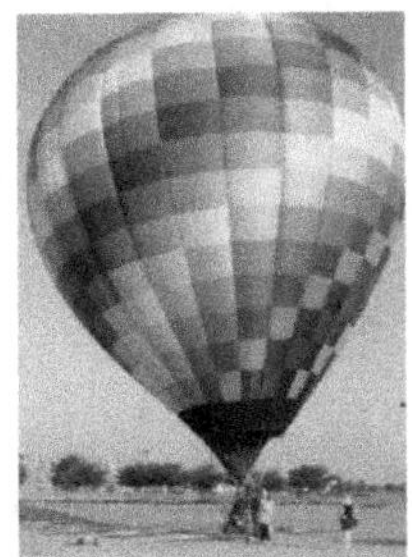

High

If you rated yourself 71-89, you are doing very well and have adopted many resiliency practices. You feel good about yourself most of the time and find yourself bouncing back from difficulties. As a learner, you find yourself looking for ways to improve and become even more resilient.

Soaring

Congratulations! At 90+, you have rated yourself very high and see yourself as very resilient. Maintaining this resilience will serve you well as you progress through the second half of your life.

Scoring Guide

1 – 50	51 – 70	71 – 89	90+
Low	Medium	High	Soaring

2 Work On It

Resilience can be learned. If you want to increase your resilience here are some ways to get started:

- Get advice from people you see as very resilient
- Learn through reading about resilient people
- Work with a personal coach to develop resiliency skills

Life after 50 is all about dealing with life changes. To have a vibrant life, we will need to be increasingly resilient. Resilient people bounce back from setbacks and find ways to make things turn out well. As Coach Vince Lombardi once said, "It isn't whether you get knocked down. It's whether you get up again." Instead of collapsing in the face of change, resilient people thrive. An individual who is resilient is flexible and creative, adapts quickly, learns from all types of experiences and gains strength through adversity.

In *The Resiliency Advantage*, Dr. Al Siebert states that one can develop one's resiliency by strengthening several key characteristics, shown below. After each characteristic, describe how it applies to you, and make note of any improvements you would like to make.

Key Resiliency Characteristics

1. *Resilient individuals are playful and curious.* They ask lots of questions, and explore new developments. They have a good time almost anywhere. Like all of us, resilient individuals make mistakes and get hurt, but they often find the humor in these events.

   This characteristic of resilience applies to me in the following ways:

   I would like to improve my level of playfulness and curiosity by:

2. *Resilient individuals learn from experience.* They quickly comprehend the unexpected experience and facilitate being changed by it. They examine the lessons to learn from the experience and look for early clues that they may have ignored. Resilient people look ahead to the next time and plan what they'll do based on what they've learned.

   This characteristic of resilience applies to me in the following ways:

   I would like to improve my level of learning from experience by:

3. *Resilient individuals have solid self-esteem and self-confidence.* They count on themselves during rough times. They have well-balanced thoughts and feelings about themselves that allow them to receive both praise and constructive criticism positively. Their healthy self-esteem and self-confidence enable them to take risks without waiting for approval from others.

This characteristic of resilience applies to me in the following ways:

I would like to improve my level of self-esteem and self-confidence by:

4. *Resilient individuals express feelings honestly.* They're comfortable openly expressing anger, love, dislike, appreciation and grief. They also can choose to suppress their feelings when they believe it is best to do so.

This characteristic of resilience applies to me in the following ways:

I would like to improve my level in the honest expression of my feelings by:

5. *Resilient individuals expect things to work out well.* They're hopeful and optimistic, and have a high tolerance for ambiguity and uncertainty. They understand that there is a connection between what they expect and how well their lives go. They ask, "How can I interact with this so that things turn out well?"

This characteristic of resilience applies to me in the following ways:

I would like to improve my level of positive expectation by:

6. *Resilient individuals read others well.* They seek to understand the perspective of others, including asking themselves what others are thinking or feeling. They approach conflict by seeking a win-win solution.

This characteristic of resilience applies to me in the following ways:

I would like to improve my level of insight into others by:

Based on this review of the key characteristics of resilient people, I rate myself as:

☐ 1	☐ 2	☐ 3	☐ 4	☐ 5
Extremely Resilient	Quite Resilient	Adequately Resilient	Somewhat Resilient	Not Very Resilient

Based on what I have learned about the importance of resilience for life after 50, I want to become:

☐ 1	☐ 2	☐ 3	☐ 4	☐ 5
Extremely Resilient	Quite Resilient	Adequately Resilient	Somewhat Resilient	Not Very Resilient

For this skill, we recommend that you do some additional personal exploration about resiliency. Do some reading, and discussion with friends, family members and other people that you trust. Develop your own sense of what you'd want to change to make yourself more resilient as you age.

Think back to two or three significant life challenges and journal how you handled the events relative to the 6 characteristics of resilient people. How would (or could) you have done better? How will you incorporate these skills into future challenges involving life changes?

Make notes in your journal of what resources you'll need in order to successfully implement and sustain your desired change. Keep in mind what you have learned from previous efforts, so that you can anticipate and overcome barriers.

We've included one goal sheet below in case specific goals come to mind.

And finally, pay attention to your thinking and internal conversations on resiliency. Return to this element every once in a while, to write additional thoughts. In addition to your attitudes about getting older, resiliency is truly a foundation for handling much of what life throws at you.

Resiliency Mindset Checklist

Resilience is the ability to get up and not give up when things don't seem to go well or as planned. Developing a mindset with resilience and determination can help you acknowledge the situation and can lead you to learn from your mistakes and move forward. Here is a checklist to guide you on how to develop such a mindset:

What Needs to Be Done:

1 Start by viewing challenges as an opportunity to improve.

2 Use these challenges to learn from your mistakes and failures.

3 Define your goals and write down what needs to be done to achieve them.

4 Identify the intensity of your wants and goals so that you can prioritize your effort.

5 Commit to your goals and promise yourself to contribute all that it will take.

6 Practice self-control and personal control.

7 Develop a sense of empowerment over your life situations.

8 Think more about the things that are going well.

9 See your problems as small and it will empower you to act in a forward direction.

10 Try breaking down your issues into smaller chunks that can be acted upon quickly. You can easily see the progress of more modest goals and tasks.

11 Start eating healthy so that you can manage stress and maintain a healthy lifestyle.

What Else Can Contribute:

1 Work on building positive beliefs in your own abilities.

2   Develop a stronger social network so that you can have supportive people around you in times of crisis.

3   Start embracing change and get out of your comfort zone more often.

4   Practice flexibility as you can be better equipped to face crisis this way.

5   Stay positive and optimistic. Understand that setbacks and problems are temporary and will go soon go away.

6   Surround yourself with people who persevere.

7   Surround yourself with people who have passion and determination.

8   Work on setting up small goals that can align with your purpose in life.

Goals	Affirmation	Action I Will Take	By When

Managing Family Relationships

Family relationships change as we get older. These changes can include such realities as more available time with one's spouse, evolving relationships with adult children, and aging parents. We do all in our power to make each relationship healthy and positive.

The reality for most of us is that our primary support network involves our partner, biological family and/or in-law family. **These relationships often change at this phase of our lives,**

because we, and they, are changing. Those who want more out of life may feel the yearning for independence.

At the same time, we could be facing the situation of aging parents who need more of our time and assistance. Our children are also experiencing changes. Where some are clearly on their life's path, many need more parental support. For those of us who are grandparents, grandchildren magnetically attract every moment of our spare time.

How can we increase our independence and individual fulfillment while attending to and strengthening family relationships? This element addresses that issue.

One of the secrets of managing changing relationships is to develop the skill of balancing apparent opposites – successfully embracing seemingly different truths at the same time – such as intimacy and independence. Numerous writers have shared the benefits of this Eastern way of approaching Life, which seems to be a hallmark of wisdom itself.

Boomers may be the first generation in history to have the opportunity to accomplish this balance, and that has significant impact on the success of our primary relationships. This is the excitement of successful aging today and we believe it will become the norm for our peers.

We are learning that the changes we're experiencing are normal (and even desirable) and do not have to equate to the popularly-held belief of "midlife crisis."

Although midlife *can* be a crisis if not processed in a good way, this natural evolution does not need to be negative. In fact, it brings energy that can build each important primary relationship.

The key is open communication and, if necessary, guidance from an objective third party to help us separate what we are experiencing from what our established belief system is telling us. We are capable of building what one expert calls "Intimate Interdependence."

Let's say your adult children presume you are going to retire soon and anticipate an increase in free childcare from you – a responsibility you may not want to take on. Are you aware of this? How are you dealing with it? What if you want to relocate? Might your children experience feelings of abandonment and resentment? What if you need to help your widowed mother relocate? How do you take the many steps required to find and fund an appropriate, supportive living environment? What about downsizing that big house the kids were raised in?

These and many other challenges will face us at this stage, and we can overcome them by finding the way that works best for us. Successfully navigating this phase of your life – while being true to your desire for independence and fulfillment – is possible. It requires consistency in awareness, intent, planning, execution and management of time.

Thinking Block – Managing Family Relationships

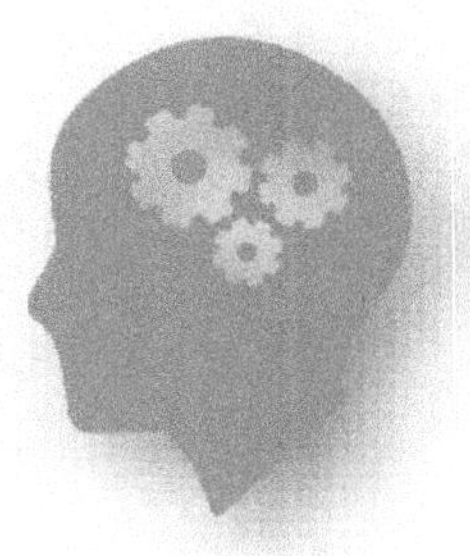

Self-Assessment - Family

This exercise is designed to help you examine your family relationships with an eye towards gauging the effectiveness of each relationship. In the first column, list everyone you consider a family member; in the next column, name their relationship to you. In the third column, rank the quality of the relationship from your perspective, using a scale of 10 (very healthy) to 1 (disengaged), and in the adjacent column to the right, check all those relationships that you would like to improve.

In the column titled "Present Caregiving," check those relationships in which you provide some form of caregiving now. In the next column, check those relationships in which you anticipate becoming a caregiver in the future.

Family Relationships Quick Assessment Tool

Name	Relationship	Quality	Would Like to Improve	Present Care-giving	Future Care-giving

<table>
<tr><td></td><td></td><td></td><td></td><td></td></tr>
<tr><td></td><td></td><td></td><td></td><td></td></tr>
<tr><td></td><td></td><td></td><td></td><td></td></tr>
<tr><td></td><td></td><td></td><td></td><td></td></tr>
<tr><td></td><td></td><td></td><td></td><td></td></tr>
<tr><td></td><td></td><td></td><td></td><td></td></tr>
<tr><td></td><td></td><td></td><td></td><td></td></tr>
</table>

> **To Carry Forward:**
> *For my family life after 50 to be as vibrant as possible, I commit to…*

Primary Relationship Questionnaire

Respond to the following statements regarding your primary relationship – the person in your life who is most important to you (e.g., spouse, significant other, close friend or family member). Circle the most appropriate number on a scale of 1 – 5 (5 = Almost Always; 1 = Almost Never).

We make intentional plans to be together.

☐ 5	☐ 4	☐ 3	☐ 2	☐ 1

We enjoy many of the same activities and entertainment.

☐ 5	☐ 4	☐ 3	☐ 2	☐ 1

We enjoy socializing with the same kinds of people.

☐ 5 ☐ 4 ☐ 3 ☐ 2 ☐ 1

We agree about our finances, and participate together on budgeting and spending decisions.

☐ 5 ☐ 4 ☐ 3 ☐ 2 ☐ 1

We are generally comfortable discussing our worries and dreams with each other.

☐ 5 ☐ 4 ☐ 3 ☐ 2 ☐ 1

There are aspects of our relationship that are too difficult to talk about.

☐ 5 ☐ 4 ☐ 3 ☐ 2 ☐ 1

I am satisfied with the affection and intimacy within our relationship.

☐ 5 ☐ 4 ☐ 3 ☐ 2 ☐ 1

I have difficulty letting go of some things that have happened in the past in our relationship.

☐ 5 ☐ 4 ☐ 3 ☐ 2 ☐ 1

We hold similar values.

☐ 5 ☐ 4 ☐ 3 ☐ 2 ☐ 1

We share similar religious beliefs.

☐ 5 ☐ 4 ☐ 3 ☐ 2 ☐ 1

We agree on the level of involvement of our extended families in our relationship.

☐ 5	☐ 4	☐ 3	☐ 2	☐ 1

My level of commitment to this relationship is best described as (check the most appropriate description):

Fully committed	Somewhat committed	Not very committed	Ready to call it quits

Rate each of the following sentence completions on a scale of 1 - 5 (5 = Almost Always; 1 = Almost Never).

In my primary relationship, I…

	Listen attentively, even when I have something important to say.
	Express my feelings accurately, using "I" messages.
	Do what I say I will do.
	Allow the other person to express her/his own views, thoughts and feelings.
	Don't make assumptions.
	Remain flexible, even when we disagree.
	Negotiate to bring about compromise.

Review your responses to the entire inventory. If there are responses that surprise or concern you, what can you learn from them, and what will you do about them?

To Carry Forward:
In my primary relationship, I would like to improve:

Relating to My Adult Children

The transition from being your child's primary caregiver to being the parent of an adult child is filled with opportunities and challenges. For you, the task is to let go without losing meaningful, life-long connectedness. For your adult child, the task is to become an independent, responsible adult, while retaining a meaningful and life-long connection to you.

Use the following questions as a basis for examining your relationship with each of your adult children.

Name of adult child _______________________________________

1. Check the response (below) that most accurately describes your level of satisfaction with your relationship to this adult child.

Very satisfied	Satisfied	Generally OK	Dissatisfied	Very dissatisfied

Comment on your response:

2. If this child is married, how satisfied are you with your relationship with her/his spouse?

Very satisfied	Satisfied	Generally OK	Dissatisfied	Very dissatisfied

Comment on your response:

3. How regular are your interactions with this adult child?

Very satisfied	Satisfied	Generally OK	Dissatisfied	Very dissatisfied

Comment on your response:

4. Complete the following sentence:

In order for my relationship with this child to be all that I would like it to be, I will need to…

Name of adult child ____

1. Check the response (below) that most accurately describes your level of satisfaction with your relationship to this adult child.

Very satisfied	Satisfied	Generally OK	Dissatisfied	Very dissatisfied

Comment on your response:

2. If this child is married, how satisfied are you with your relationship with her/his spouse?

Very satisfied	Satisfied	Generally OK	Dissatisfied	Very dissatisfied

Comment on your response:

3. How regular are your interactions with this adult child?

Very satisfied	Satisfied	Generally OK	Dissatisfied	Very dissatisfied

Comment on your response:

4. Complete the following sentence:

In order for my relationship with this child to be all that I would like it to be, I will need to…

Name of adult child ____

1. Check the response (below) that most accurately describes your level of satisfaction with your relationship to this adult child.

Very satisfied	Satisfied	Generally OK	Dissatisfied	Very dissatisfied

Comment on your response:

2. If this child is married, how satisfied are you with your relationship with her/his spouse?

Very satisfied	Satisfied	Generally OK	Dissatisfied	Very dissatisfied

Comment on your response:

3. How regular are your interactions with this adult child?

Very satisfied	Satisfied	Generally OK	Dissatisfied	Very dissatisfied

Comment on your response:

4. Complete the following sentence:

In order for my relationship with this child to be all that I would like it to be, I will need to…

Name of adult child ____

1. Check the response (below) that most accurately describes your level of satisfaction with your relationship to this adult child.

Very satisfied	Satisfied	Generally OK	Dissatisfied	Very dissatisfied

Comment on your response:

2. If this child is married, how satisfied are you with your relationship with her/his spouse?

Very satisfied	Satisfied	Generally OK	Dissatisfied	Very dissatisfied

Comment on your response:

3. How regular are your interactions with this adult child?

Very satisfied	Satisfied	Generally OK	Dissatisfied	Very dissatisfied

Comment on your response:

4. Complete the following sentence:

In order for my relationship with this child to be all that I would like it to be, I will need to…

Check the most appropriate answer to the following questions.

As an adult child myself, my relationship with my parents is/was:

	Excellent
	Mostly good
	Somewhat difficult
	Very difficult
	I don't/didn't have an adult relationship with my parents

I worry about my adult children's welfare:

	All of the time
	Often
	Sometimes
	Hardly ever

I like the amount of time I spend with my adult children.

	Very satisfied
	Satisfied
	Dissatisfied
	Very dissatisfied

My adult children still need financial assistance from me.

	All of the time
	Often
	Sometimes
	Hardly ever

I feel taken advantage of by my adult children.

	All of the time
	Often
	Sometimes
	Hardly ever

To Carry Forward:
In order to improve my relationships with my adult children, I commit to:

If My Adult Child Comes Home

It is not uncommon for adult children to return home after being on their own for a while. In fact, the U.S. Census Bureau reports that 27% of people between the ages of 18 and 34 live with a parent. But much about life at home has changed since they moved out. So, it's important to discuss expectations, decide on what the arrangement today will be and reach mutual agreement with the parties involved. It becomes all the more important if there are "step" relationships involved (stepchild/stepparent).

Write a response to each question.

Will my adult child pay rent? If so, what's reasonable?

As an adult member of the household, what household maintenance activities will be expected of my adult child (e.g., laundry, cleaning, snow removal and yard work)?

What are my expectations regarding groceries, cooking and meals?

What are my wants around privacy, noise level, visitors and stay-over guests?

If my adult child is staying out overnight, what are my expectations regarding communication?

Is there a time limit on my adult child living with me?

To what extent is my spouse, partner or roommate aware of and in agreement with these desires?

What of the above information has been communicated to my adult child?

In the space below, draft a written agreement that you could use with your adult child to make certain that your expectations are clear, and to minimize avoidable conflicts.

What has surprised you about completing this exercise?

To Carry Forward:
In order to make certain that "boomerang" children don't negatively impact the vibrancy of my life after 50, I commit to:

Caregiving for My Aging Parents

Caring for one's aging parent(s) can range from doing simple tasks, such as snow removal or balancing the check book, to around-the-clock nursing care. Wherever on that continuum you are or ultimately may be, it is likely that you'll encounter emotional, physical and financial challenges as your parent(s) move through the later stages of their lives. Take the time to explore what kind of a caregiver you want to be for your aging parents.

Using a scale of 10 (high) to 1 (low), how would you rate your current relationship with your parent(s)? Note any personal comments or thoughts about this rating for you.

LOW   **HIGH**

☐ 1	☐ 2	☐ 3	☐ 4	☐ 5	☐ 6	☐ 7	☐ 8	☐ 9	☐ 10

Comments:

Using the same scale, how *satisfied* are you with this current relationship? Note any personal comments or thoughts about this level of satisfaction for you.

LOW   **HIGH**

☐ 1	☐ 2	☐ 3	☐ 4	☐ 5	☐ 6	☐ 7	☐ 8	☐ 9	☐ 10

Comments:

On the same scale, how motivated/committed are you to wanting to change this? Note any personal comments or thoughts about this level of commitment to change for you.

LOW   **HIGH**

☐ 1	☐ 2	☐ 3	☐ 4	☐ 5	☐ 6	☐ 7	☐ 8	☐ 9	☐ 10

Comments:

Check all the areas in which you want to provide support for your parent(s):

	Area of Support
	Companionship
	House upkeep chores (e.g., yard maintenance, minor home repairs)
	Grocery shopping
	Personal shopping; clothing, etc.
	Arranging and accompanying to doctors, dental, eye glass appointments
	House cleaning, laundry and the like
	Bill paying and banking
	Transportation
	Personal care (dressing, bathing)
	Researching and arranging for an alternative residence (e.g., nursing home)
	In-home care (<u>your</u> home)
	Other:

How will you determine the needs of your parent/s as they evolve?

How will you be clear about what your own needs are? How will you assess your own needs?

What are the family dynamics that might help with caregiving of your parents?

What are the family dynamics that might complicate the caregiving of your parents?

If you have taken on caregiving responsibilities, or anticipate that you may be called upon for this role, what specific things will you do to take care of yourself in the process and to maintain a positive attitude? What are your options? What resources are available to help you?

What barriers may exist between you and your parent/s?

What, specifically, can you do to help break down those barriers?

What is important for you to accomplish with your parent(s) before they die?

What steps do you need to take *now* to ensure that you accomplish the things of importance that you have identified?

To Carry Forward:
In order to be appropriately responsible to my aging parent(s) and to myself throughout my life after 50, I commit to:

Work On It

And now it's time to summarize your goals and actions.

- *Write as specifically as you can your desired behavior change (goal). You may want to use the SMART goal methodology for this (Specific, Measurable, Achievable, Realistic and Timely). For example, a SMART goal would be: "Call my mother at least once a week, starting now". You may want to identify more than one desired change.*

- *Write a motivation statement (affirmation) that you can return to as a reminder of why that behavior change is important to you.*

Goals	Affirmation	Action I Will Take	By When

Congratulations! You've wrestled with some significant questions and have the beginnings of a plan to help you create a vibrant life after 50 with the Family element. It's a good stopping point with this element for now. Your next task is to take the actions that you promised yourself. Truthfully, your work here is only just beginning. Revisit this section as you need, and evaluate how you're doing against your goals.

It's a great time to discuss your goals, plans, and learnings with your family. Here are journal pages where you can write about anything that comes to mind regarding this topic. We'll see you in the next section!

Building A Social Network

Our support system is essential, energizing and fulfilling. It's important to grow our social networks.

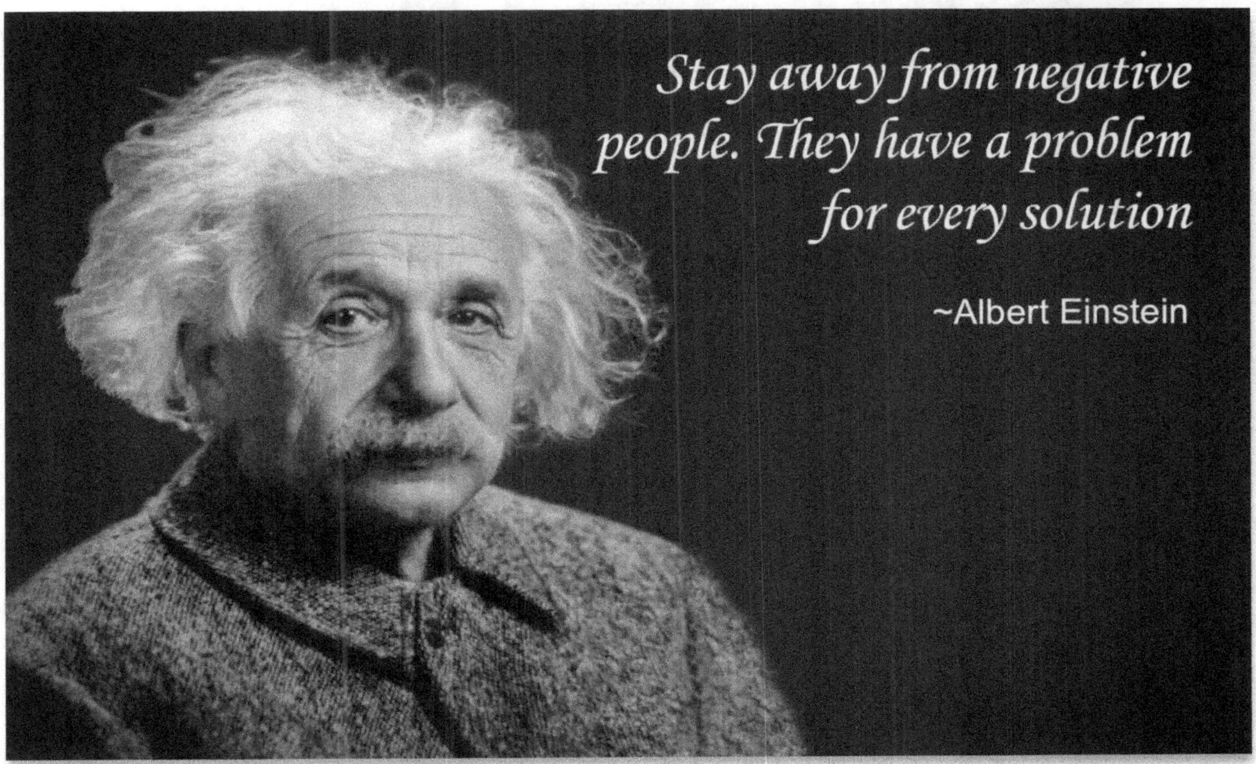

Believe it or not, the strength of your support system is a greater predictor of life satisfaction than either wealth or health. Indeed, studies show that people who interact regularly with others live healthier, happier, longer lives. Developing and maintaining one's social network, therefore, is a critical challenge for those over 50, whether planning imminent retirement, or simply moving into the middle years mindfully.

Think about the importance of your social network in the light of these points:

Work is the most common source of friendships and socialization—not surprising when we consider the many hours spent with coworkers.

If retirement is chosen, work-based relationships typically dissipate. The retiree is no longer a part of the daily break-room conversations, nor a participant in work-related problem-solving and successes.

When we choose to change, "upgrade," or otherwise redefine our jobs, many of us also choose to relocate, which adds the complexity of distance to the task of maintaining current friendships.

It takes considerable and intentional time and effort to establish friendships. Rather than discouraging you, these realities of your life after 50 can motivate you to examine the current state of your own social network. Do you have good friends and acquaintances?

When we reflect on the fact that we spend more time each week at work than in any other single environment, it isn't any wonder that work is a primary source of social networking for many people. **As we consider the possibility of moving out of the workplace, however, it's important to anticipate that some of these relationships may change.** Over time, they may become less strong through lack of support and less frequent contact. In fact, for some who will choose a traditional retirement and relocate to a new community, relationships established at work may well come to an end.

As you look to ensure a vibrant life after 50 for yourself, you'll want to examine the role of the workplace in your current social network. **If it has been the most important one, you need to anticipate changes in those relationships over the coming years, and develop a plan for building your social network outside of the workplace.** Remember that establishing lasting relationships takes time.

Start building your social network immediately so you'll be prepared and thus avoid the loneliness and pain that so many endure. Our social network – our "chosen family" – is a wonderful asset to successful aging and will prove to be a great comfort as these good years unfold, regardless of any other middle life choices.

Fortunately, people have more tools and options today than ever before to accomplish this goal. There are social networks, social media groups, faith-based organizations, health and leisure organizations, travel and adventure options, cooking clubs…how many have you seen or heard of?

Do you participate in any of these networks? We have choices today, through focused planning and action, to participate in meaningful and enjoyable ways that bring us a sense of fulfillment.

As you negotiate life after 50, we hope you'll identify the unique social preferences, aptitudes and interests you (and your partner) possess. Then, plan and develop them to the fullest. Whether on your own, through clubs and social networks, or by using resources such as coaching services, successful members of our generation will study, plan and build connections to support their interests.

Thinking Block – Building a Social Network Outside of Work

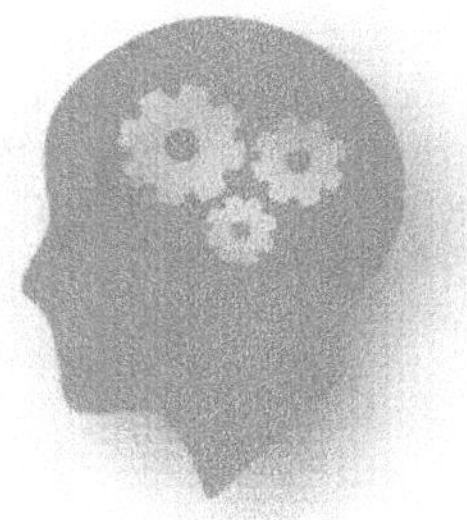

Self-Assessment – Building your Social Network Outside of Work

Review the list below.

Check all the places where you have met people. Add any others that have been important people-meeting places in your life.

For each place you checked, think about the people you've met there and the relationships that have resulted. In the right-hand column, categorize the types of relationships that have developed from each identified non-work venue. Use consistent categories, such as Casual acquaintances, Good acquaintances, Good friendships and Close friendships.

	Location	Types of Relationships
	Work	
	Adult Education classes	
	Faith community	
	Political organization	
	Neighborhood	
	Children's activities	
	Social organization	

	Location	Types of Relationships
	Volunteer activity	
	Facebook/Internet	
	Club or bar	
	Health club	
	Hobby club	
	Other:	
	Other:	
	Other:	

In which places and circumstances did you meet people with whom your relationships have evolved into friendships or good acquaintances?

What do these places and circumstances share in common?

What have you learned from this regarding where you might expand your social network in the future?

List below any other places where you would feel comfortable meeting new people today.

What personal attributes make it easier for you to meet people?

What gets in your way of getting to know new people?

What can you do so that your people-meeting strengths overcome your barriers to getting to know new people?

What personal attributes do you look for in a friend?

What will you do today, this week and this year to strengthen those social relationships that will remain after you've left the workplace?

To Carry Forward:
In order to expand and strengthen my social network, I commit to...

Work On It

And now it's time to summarize your goals and actions.

- *Write as specifically as you can your desired behavior change (goal). You may want to use the SMART goal methodology for this (Specific, Measurable, Achievable, Realistic and Timely). For example, a SMART goal would be: "Invite one person to coffee once per month beginning in January". You may want to identify more than one desired change.*
- *Write a motivation statement (affirmation) that you can return to as a reminder of why that behavior change is important to you.*

Goals	Affirmation	Action I Will Take	By When

Living a Meaningful Life

*As we look back at our lives and forward to these
coming years, we crave a deepening sense of meaning*

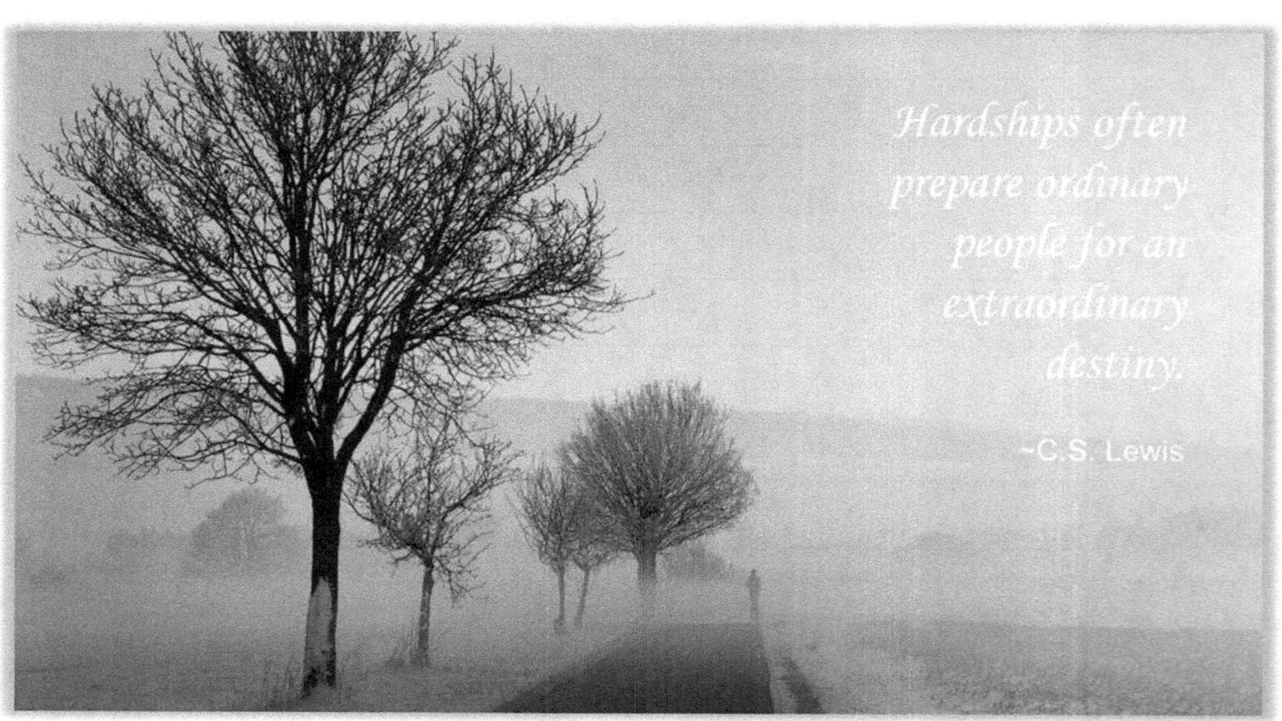

What gets you up and going in the morning? OK, it's still the alarm clock. But what would awaken you to life each new day – day after day – if you decided to change your routine?

- If you take that course at the University?
- If you teach that course?
- If you volunteer with that non-profit (or start one)?
- If you join that travel/adventure group or go to new places?

Conduct a personal inventory of your unique life incentives. As you enter this time of your life, become aware of what motivates you – or, as in the common expression, what "trips your trigger?" **This will ensure that your days will center on activities that bring you meaning and keep you from the trap of the "same old, same old.**

A Word to the Wise:

We have such opportunity for achieving unprecedented fulfillment. We must examine any detrimental patterns of thinking, feeling and acting. Identify what inspires and motivates you. You'll be able to plan for a purposeful and meaningful life after 50 – a life that actively meets your deepest wants and needs, long after you've stashed away your alarm clock!

Some people already have clearly identified motivators. These are often the activities that they do now in the evenings and on weekends, and around which they plan their vacations. These include, for example, hobbies, volunteerism, physical activity, part-time work or the development of a start-up business. **However, even these people would do well to ask themselves, "Will these same activities fulfill me as I get older, or when I retire and have significantly more time? Or is there more to me I have yet to discover?"**

Others aren't accustomed to giving a lot of thought to ideas like "fulfillment," "purpose" or "life meaning." At this point in their lives, these people already know what they like, and they look forward to spending more time on those things as they age, without delving further into whether there's anything more to life.

After you do your personal inventory, we suggest that you share it with a significant person in your life, and work your plan in clear, measurable steps. When you look back over a year of journaling your growth, you may well be amazed at the growth you've experienced.

Gratitude

An important part of a meaningful life is to adopt an attitude of gratitude. Many people spend their entire lives without realizing how grateful they could be for the things in life they've already been blessed with.

When your feet hit the floor in the morning, find something to be grateful for and carry it with you throughout the day. This works especially well for the small, simple things in life – the warmth of the sunshine, a baby's smile, clean water to drink, friends, a coworker's interesting story, etc.

Sincere gratitude brings an appreciation of people and life around us and helps shut out some of the all too common negativity in the world. In short, by itself, an attitude of gratitude makes life more meaningful.

Before we get into the exercises to find meaning in life, spend some time on the Gratitude Diagram on the next page. And each day afterward, reflect on one or more of them in the morning, or at night before sleep. Doing so can make a huge difference in your outlook in life as well as contribute to your mental and physical health.

Consistently doing this simple act is noticeable to those around you – *and highly contagious!*

Gratitude Diagram

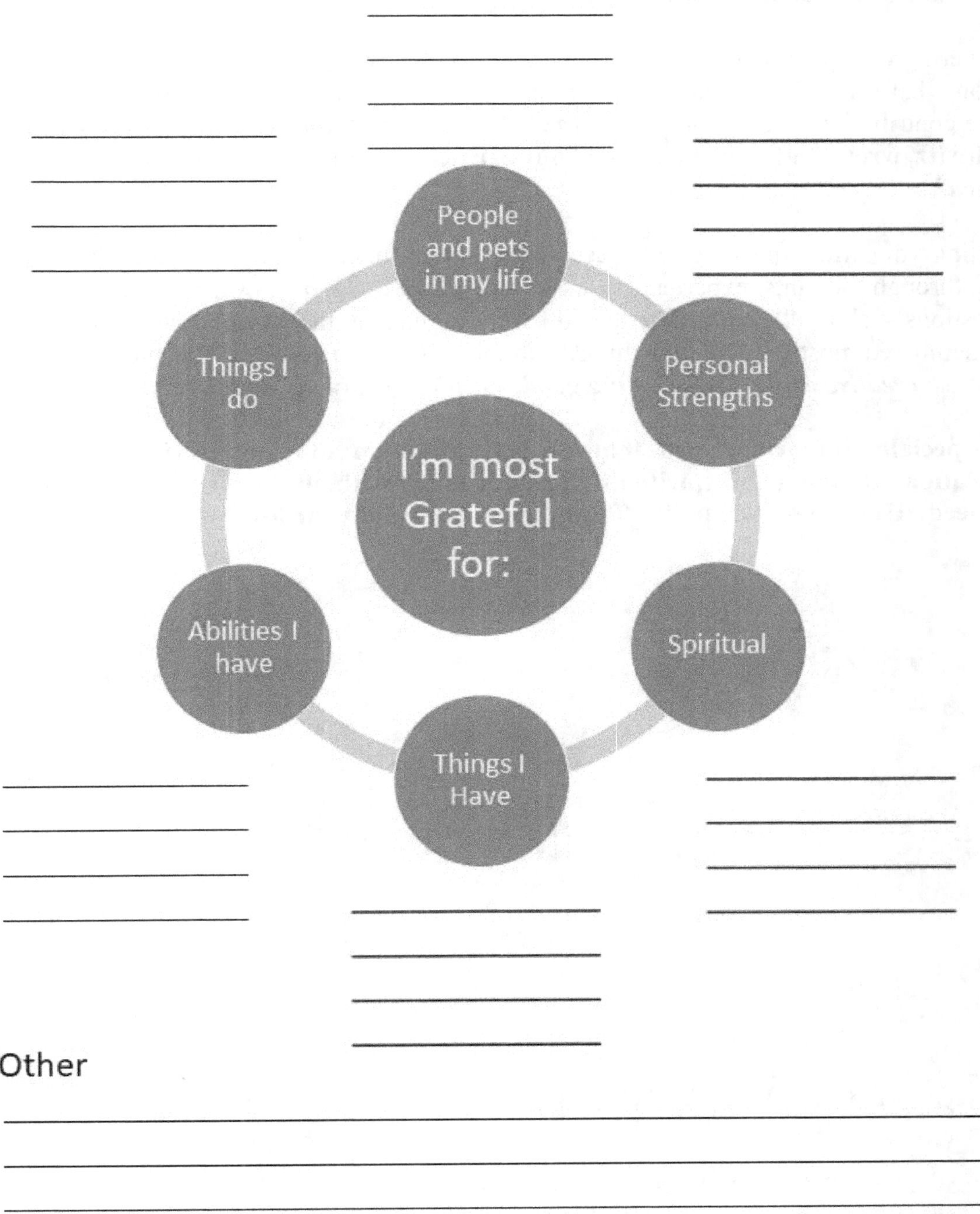

Other

Finding Life's Meaning and Purpose

Everyone has a unique purpose in life, often referred to as life meaning, even *passion*. That purpose may or may not be the same as our work. In fact, highly accomplished professionals often discover their life purpose outside of their work. In any case, each of us must discover our own passion so that we can live out that purpose.

Discovering your passion is a highly individualized task. It's *your* life's purpose. No one else can tell you what it is. Others may, however, enlighten you as to how to go about discovering your unique contribution to the world. **In *Man's Search for Meaning*, Viktor Frankl, survivor of Auschwitz, wrote that "the meaning of our existence is not invented by ourselves, but rather, detected."**

Detecting your life's meaning will necessitate thoughtful effort on your part. It's a process of sifting through thoughts, experiences, losses and regrets, to arrive, ever more closely, at answers to questions such as, "What difference do I want to make in the world?" and "What do I want to be remembered most for accomplishing?" In the following exercises, you'll explore meaning in five areas: *creative expression, finding good, spirituality, giving, and dreams*.

It's especially important also that we pay attention to your spiritual nature in this exploration. Religion and spirituality provide many with all the meaning in life that they'll ever need. How does spirituality fit into the meaning of your life?

Thinking Block – Living a Meaningful Life

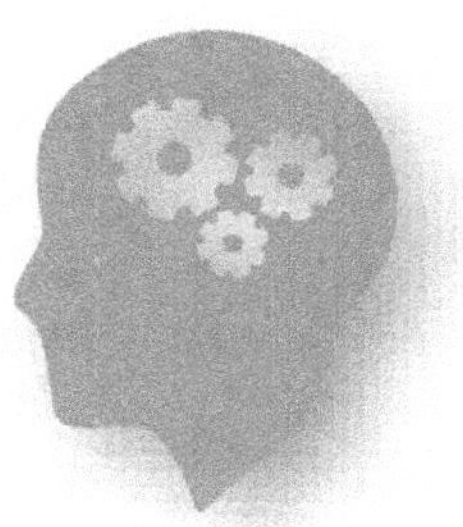

Self-Assessment – Living a Meaningful Life

Creative expression – List three ways you have experienced your inner self in creative ways, and how this has benefited you.

Personal Experiences of Creative Expression	Benefits

<u>Finding good</u> – List three ways or examples of times you unexpectedly found goodness or beauty in the world or within yourself. How did each affect you?

Personal Experiences of Finding Good	Effects

<u>Spirituality</u> – It's a fact that human beings have a spiritual nature. No matter what your religion or beliefs, it's important that we develop that side of our nature. List your three strongest spiritual beliefs or experiences.

Spiritual Belief or Experience	How It Improves My Life

<u>Giving</u> – a meaningful life is often characterized by what you give to others and to the world. List anything that you would want to give to your family, community, or the world, e.g. time, expertise, ideas, money, joy, etc.

Gift	To Whom

Dreams – *List everything you want to do, to go to, to have, to be, to become. Throw out the filters of whether you need it, deserve it, or are worth it. This is an exercise in dreaming.*

My Dreams

Based on this brief inner journey, what have you learned regarding your life's meaning or purpose?

How will you apply what you've learned? That is, what will you do, specifically, and how will you be different in the world as a result of these insights into your purpose and meaning?

To Carry Forward:
Building on what I have discovered, I want to continue on my quest for my life meaning by:

Work On It

Writing My Personal Mission Statement

"The key to the ability to change is a changeless sense of who you are, what you are about and what you value." – Stephen R. Covey

---

Companies often create mission statements that define an organization's values and goals. The statement is then used to make decisions and define business practices. People benefit from writing a personal mission statement, a written expression of their values and life goals.

This is a uniquely personal process. There is no set formula for writing a personal mission statement. But, as with businesses, a personal mission statement can stand as a reminder of the life you want to lead and a guide for decision-making in your future.

Here are some questions to get you started:

What qualities do you most admire in others?

What kind of person do you want to be?

What are your greatest personal strengths?

What are your guiding moral principles?

What values do you consider most important? List the top three.

What relationships do you value most?

What activities give you the greatest satisfaction?

How do you define success?

When you die, what do you want people to remember most about you?

What additional thoughts are important to writing your personal mission statement?

Now it's time to begin crafting your personal mission statement. It is a statement that will not flow from you, fully formed. You'll need to revise your mission statement several times. To that end, we encourage you to carry your statement with you. That will help you keep it in the forefront of your thinking, making it easier for you to note changes until the statement describes the best that you are today, and the best that you hope to become in your life after 50.

You can use the following page for notes as you develop your personal mission statement.

My Personal Mission Statement

> ### To Carry Forward:
>
> To live my mission, I need a clear statement of my mission.
> To that end, I commit to:

And now summarize any goals or actions.

- *Write as specifically as you can your desired behavior change (goal). You may want to use the SMART goal methodology for this (Specific, Measurable, Achievable, Realistic and Timely). For example, a SMART goal would be: "I will meditate daily for 15 minutes per day beginning tomorrow". You may want to identify more than one desired change.*

- *Write a motivation statement (affirmation) that you can return to as a reminder of why that behavior change is important to you.*

Goals	Affirmation	Action I Will Take	By When

Congratulations! You've wrestled with some significant questions and have the beginnings of a plan to help you create a vibrant life after 50 with the Meaningful Life element. It's a good stopping point with this element for now. Your next task is to take the actions that you promised yourself. Truthfully, your work here is only just beginning. Revisit this section as you need, and evaluate how you're doing against your goals.

It's a great time to discuss your goals, plans and learnings with friends and family. Here are journal pages where you can write about anything that comes to mind regarding this topic. We'll see you in the next section!

Ensuring a Balanced Life

We have expended much energy over the years in our careers and find that this is a time when we choose to balance "doing" with "being", adding a sense of greater enjoyment.

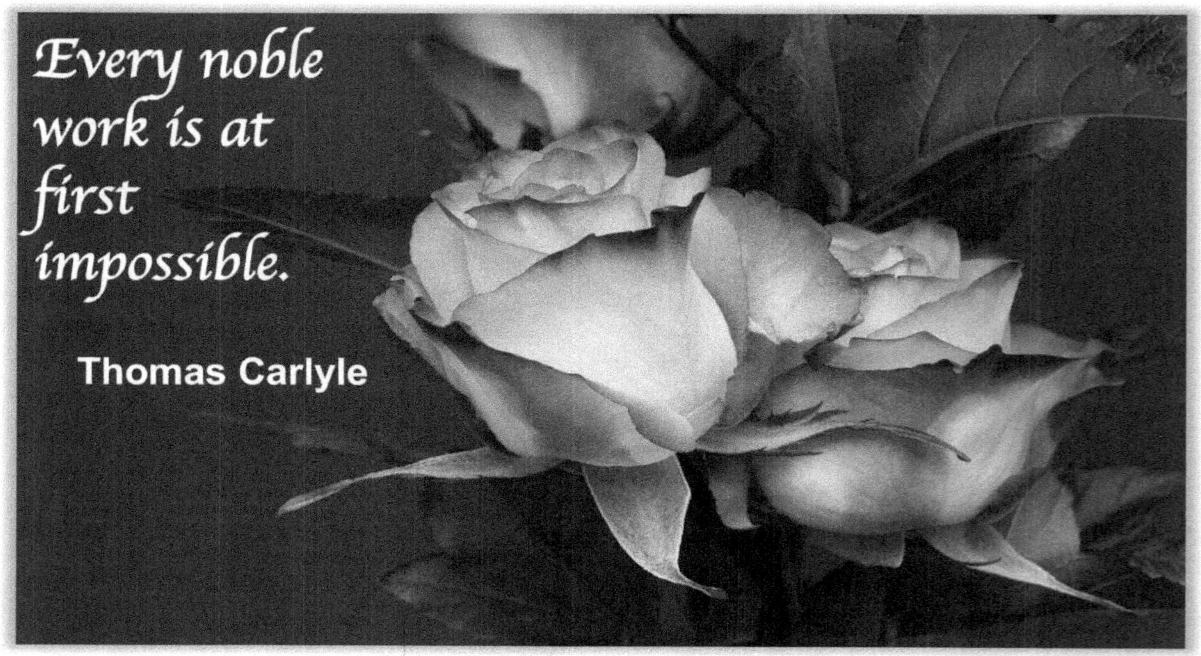

We like to say that this wonderful time in our lives is about living a leisurely life, not a life of leisure. We don't want to be rushed or bothered. **We DO want to commit to something we believe in, and live with the joyful energy that comes from knowing we are doing what we believe is right and good for us.** A key to doing this successfully after 50 is to participate in physical and mental activities that renew us, and doing so in ways that rejuvenate us.

Since employment consumes approximately 45% or more of our available awake time each week, it's no wonder so many of us eagerly anticipate a time for more leisure – more "free time." And yet, there are two potholes to be aware of:

Leisure can actually be a potential barrier to a vibrant life after 50.

Many of us don't want to retire; we just want to spend our time in self-directed, meaningful ways.

In a recent poll, 41% of retirees cited monotony and boredom as the most difficult part of their retired life. Think of that! Four in 10 retirees suffering from too much free time!

To retain its revitalizing value, leisure must remain as a contrast to some sort of daily routine, long before retirement comes. For example, when Clara retired, she moved to a retirement community in the south. She played golf every morning and cards every afternoon – the two things she'd always most enjoyed on weekends and vacations during her working years.

From working with our clients, we believe people are really suffering from a failure to understand leisure.

At first, life was better than ever for Clara. But in a short time, she became noticeably unhappy and she complained more frequently of aches and illnesses. Clara had transformed her leisure activities – those things that had been her break from routine – into routine activities themselves.

What she now needed was to create leisure in her life by identifying new, pleasurable activities as a break from her new routine of golf and cards. And she also needed to become more "leisurely" in her approach to golf and cards, by perhaps intentionally limiting these activities to three or four times a week.

Does this sound familiar? How many of us have talked about having to take a vacation from vacation? We know that through examination of your leisure preferences and existing habits, and implementing a personalized leisure plan into your daily life, you can create a leisurely way of living that satisfies your deepest needs.

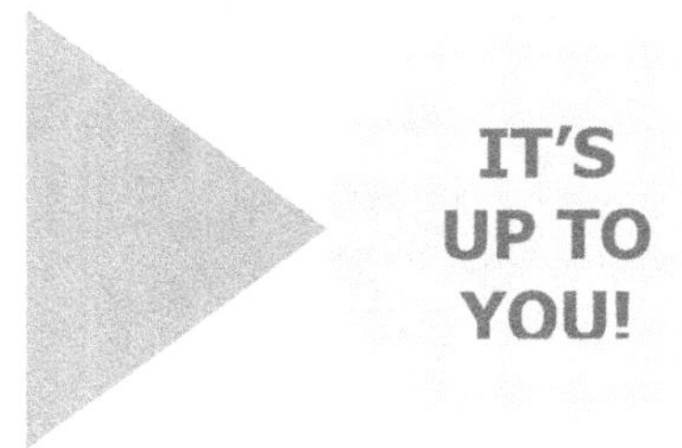

As you make choices related to significant changes in your work routine, you alone will **decide if your life will be one of leisure, with its potential for monotony and boredom, or one that is full and meaningful, yet lived at a leisurely pace.** It's an important distinction.

Another great option is for people in this situation to start their own business. Bloomberg.com recently reported the following: *"Starting a business during the traditional retirement years is rising: 55 to 64-year-olds accounted for 26% of new entrepreneurs in 2017, up from 15% in 1996.*

The reasons for this trend are many, but primarily, online skills and tools make it easier to start a business. In addition, as we pointed out earlier, retirement is not an option for many people, and **what better way to create an income then by leveraging in-demand skills and experiences that took years to build?**

If and when you make changes that leave you with more free time on your hands, thoughtful planning will help you navigate the transition from time previously scheduled for you, to time used at your own discretion, doing the things you truly want to do, in the company of those with whom you wish to spend your precious time.

Leisure is vital to life balance. It provides us with a break in the routine of our lives. While we work, leisure is a clear change from the demands of our jobs and careers, and primarily occurs on weekends and vacations. For those who retire or move to alternative work arrangements, leisure time increases measurably, making all the more important the identification of activities that are enjoyable, satisfying and lasting, and that promote leisurely living.

Thinking Block – Living a Balanced Life

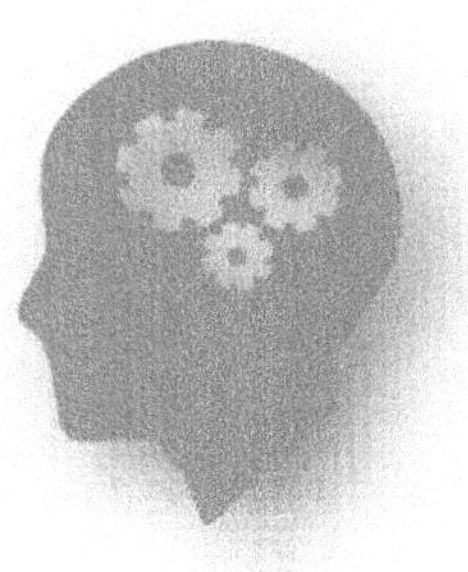

Your Wheel of Life

1 How balanced is your life?

To find out, place a dot at the appropriate spot within each of the eight sections of the circle below, using the center of the circle as "0" (totally unsatisfied with where I am) and the outer edge as "10" (totally satisfied with where I am).

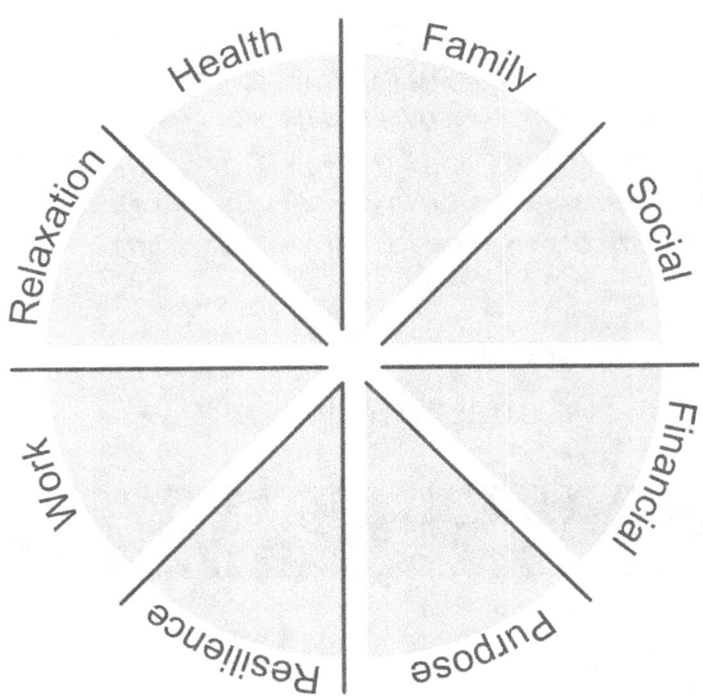

Now, use a red pencil to draw a line connecting the dots within the adjacent sections. How balanced is your wheel of life today? How "bumpy" would your ride be, if this was a real wheel?

Now place a dot at the appropriate spot within each of the eight sections based on where you are determined to be one year from today (using the same value rankings). Using a green pencil, draw a line connecting these dots. Does your Wheel of life look more balanced? What specific steps will you commit to taking, in order to achieve better balance by one year from today?

For the purposes of this next exercise, we have categorized leisure activities as spectator, intellectual, creative, social, physical and solitary. Each table in this exercise addresses one of these categories and includes examples of leisure activities. Neither the categories nor the activities are exhaustive or complete, but can serve as starting points for you to modify for your situation.

For each category:

- *In the left-hand column, cross off those activities that hold no interest for you. Write in the empty spaces any additional activities that interest you and that you might consider for your leisure time in the future. Don't be overly concerned about properly categorizing these additional activities.*
- *In the next column, write in an estimate of the amount of time you currently spend in that particular activity. Please select a measure to use consistently throughout this exercise (e.g., hours per week or month).*
- *In the third column, project as realistically as you can how much time you would like to dedicate to each activity in the future.*

Spectator Activities

Activities	Time Spent Currently	Projected Time Spent
Sporting events		
Theater		

Activities	Time Spent Currently	Projected Time Spent
Symphony		
Movies		
Museums		
Opera/ballet		
Time Totals		

Intellectual Activities

Activities	Time Spent Currently	Projected Time Spent
Adult education classes		
College or university courses		
Study groups		
Book/reading groups		
Learning another language		
Computer and Mobile skills		
Time Totals		

Creative Activities

Activities	Time Spent Currently	Projected Time Spent
Acting		
Music		
Writing		
Painting		
Storytelling		
Woodworking		
Time Totals		

Social Activities

Activities	Time Spent Currently	Projected Time Spent
Entertaining		
Volunteerism		
Faith community		
Politics		
Group travel		
Hobby club		
Elder hostels		
Social media engagement		
Time Totals		

Physical Activities

Activities	Time Spent Currently	Projected Time Spent
Group sports		
Hiking		
Biking		
Kayaking		
Golf		
Sailing		
Time Totals		

Solitary Activities

Activities	Time Spent Currently	Projected Time Spent
Meditation		
Photography		
Reading		
Word puzzles/Sudoku		
Television		
Journaling		
Time Totals		

Now go back and total the time totals for both your current and projected leisure activities:

Total Time Spent Currently:

Total Projected Time Spent:

How do the totals compare?

How adequately does your projected amount of time spent in leisure activities 10 years from now address any anticipated decrease in time spent at work?

What can you learn from this exercise regarding the place of leisure in your life today and as you project it to be in 10 years?

> *To Carry Forward:*
> *To add the benefit of leisurely living to my life after 50, I commit to...*

Work On It

And now it's time to summarize any goals or actions.

- *Write as specifically as you can your desired behavior change (goal). You may want to use the SMART goal methodology for this (Specific, Measurable, Achievable, Realistic and Timely). For example, a SMART goal would be: "I will meditate daily for 15 minutes per day beginning tomorrow". You may want to identify more than one desired change.*

- *Write a motivation statement (affirmation) that you can return to as a reminder of why that behavior change is important to you.*

Goals	Affirmation	Action I Will Take	By When

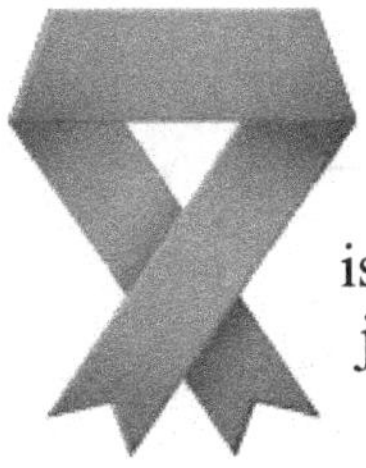 Congratulations! You've wrestled with some significant questions and have the beginnings of a plan to help you create a vibrant life after 50 with the Meaningful Life element. It's a good stopping point with this element for now. Your next task is to take the actions that you promised yourself. Truthfully, your work here is only just beginning. Revisit this section as you need, and evaluate how you're doing against your goals.

It's a great time to discuss your goals, plans, and learnings with friends and family. Here are journal pages where you can write about anything that comes to mind regarding this topic. We'll see you in the next section!

Working Your Finances

There are many things to be prepared for during life after 50 that have financial implications, whether or not it is time to retire.

Our journey would not be complete without an element of financial security. A successful executive recently stated, "Making the adjustment to retirement (financial independence) is one of the most difficult transitions facing Americans." This is a clear, simple perspective that true retirement cannot occur without financial independence.

In addition, everyone, whether retired or not, has to figure out how to afford their health and lifestyle as they age. For the well-off, investments and passive income will be more than enough to see their life through comfortably. But the majority of people will struggle with the twin swords of increasing prices, and reduced – or no earning power.

We believe having a financial plan that instills confidence can give you the freedom to focus on all of the other Elements of a successful life at this age, while preparing for retirement, when or if you choose. Without it, each of the other Elements can be much more of a struggle and the choices severely restricted.

Your financial future is one of those areas where it is best to seek advice from an attorney, financial planner, or accountant. Elder attorneys are great resources that combine specialized elder law, financial knowledge, and the perspective of aging.

Your individualized financial plan should include projected needs and resources.

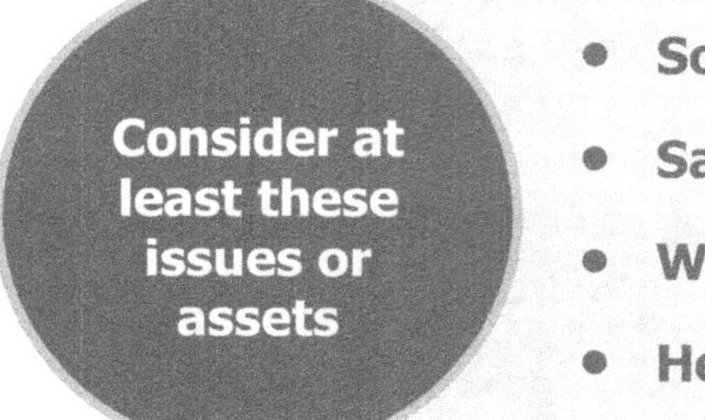

Each of us needs a life plan, a clear vision of the big picture. For most of us, great benefit is found in obtaining professional guidance so that the major pieces of our financial lives fit together easily and comfortably.

If you're looking for a financial professional, here are some important questions to ask candidates:

1   **What is your background and past financial services experience?**

2   **What type of professional education/advanced credentials do you have? What licenses do you have, and in what geographic areas (states; provinces) are you licensed?**

3   **Tell me about your support team. Who assists you? Whom do I contact if you are unreachable?**

4   **Describe your typical client. Is this "typical client" similar or dissimilar to me?**

5   **How do you service your advice and/or the products/services that I purchase?**

6 **What does an ongoing relationship look like and what are any ongoing fees or costs?**

Seek advice early on your Social Security and Medicare options. This advice can be obtained for free. And it is well worth it to discuss with an expert the benefit and timing of taking Social Security benefits. Many times, there are benefits that you wouldn't know about. Knowing ahead of time the best way to combine your work benefits and financial assets with Social Security.

Most members of the Boomer generation have the potential to live out a life that no previous generation could have imagined. To realize the fulfillment we all deserve, a critical starting point is financial independence.

Thinking Block – Working Your Finances

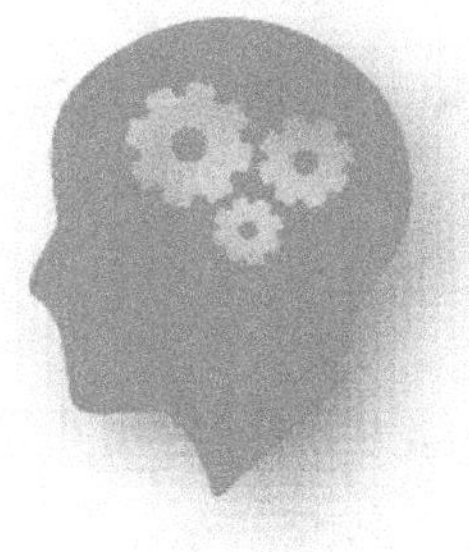

Financial Self-Assessment

1 *Please answer each question about your "financial readiness" for the future, whether or not you envision the traditional definition of "retirement" for your life after 50. Circle the number in the right-hand column that corresponds to your response (1 = No concern/Fully addressed; 5 = Highly concerned/Needs to be addressed).*

Financial Self-Assessment	
I'm concerned about outliving my money.	1 2 3 4 5
I have a monthly budget.	1 2 3 4 5
I live within my budget.	1 2 3 4 5
I am able to save money for my future.	1 2 3 4 5
I have good credit.	1 2 3 4 5
I'm concerned what market corrections would do to my financial resources.	1 2 3 4 5
My income is invested appropriately based on my timeline and risk tolerance.	1 2 3 4 5
I have identified a tax-efficient manner to withdraw income, as needed, throughout my future.	1 2 3 4 5
My future income needs are "inflation-proof."	1 2 3 4 5
I feel my future income will need to be supported with hobby income or part-time employment.	1 2 3 4 5
I have a strategy in place to address long-term care needs.	1 2 3 4 5
I have prepared written directives in the event of incapacity or terminal illness.	1 2 3 4 5
My will and trust are up to date.	1 2 3 4 5
I have determined a tax-efficient strategy for the distribution of my estate.	1 2 3 4 5
I have established a legacy – a written plan to carry on my financial contributions to causes, pursuits, charitable and/or religious organizations, educational pursuits, etc., beyond my lifetime.	1 2 3 4 5
I know the amount of income I need to support my future lifestyle.	1 2 3 4 5
I know what income to expect from Social Security, company pensions, and personal investments.	1 2 3 4 5
I'll need to supplement my income after I retire or get laid off	1 2 3 4 5
My spouse/significant other/partner and I agree on a clear financial plan for our future and mutually understand the plan.	1 2 3 4 5
I have a plan to minimize estate taxes (if applicable), inheritance tax, probate costs, and a plan to equalize my estate for loved ones.	1 2 3 4 5

I am "fully confident and ready" with my financial planning for the future.	**1 2 3 4 5**

Review your assessment, in particular noting any statements where you have circled a 3, 4 or 5. In the space below, note those areas of a comprehensive financial plan to which you still need to attend.

If you are in a primary relationship (spouse, significant other, legal partner), to what extent have you shared the details of your financial plan (1 = Not at all; 5 = Fully shared)?

☐ 5	☐ 4	☐ 3	☐ 2	☐ 1

If you have checked anything other than 5, note below your reasons for not sharing your financial plan fully, within your primary relationship. How does this relate to the Addressing Family Issues Element of your plan for a vibrant life after 50?

Now summarize what you believe are your financial strengths and weaknesses, and how important you think these are as you move through your 50's, 60's and beyond.

My Main Financial Strengths	How Important Will This Be?

My Main Financial Weaknesses Are	How Important Will This Be?

> **To Carry Forward:**
> *In my financial plan, I would like to improve...*

Work On It

And now it's time to summarize any goals or actions.

- *Write as specifically as you can your desired behavior change (goal). You may want to use the SMART goal methodology for this (Specific, Measurable, Achievable, Realistic and Timely). For example, a SMART goal would be: "I will create a will by June 1". You may want to identify more than one desired change.*
- *Write a motivation statement (affirmation) that you can return to as a reminder of why that behavior change is important to you.*

Goals	Affirmation	Action I Will Take	By When

 Congratulations! You've wrestled with some significant questions and have the beginnings of a plan to help you create a vibrant life after 50 with the Financial element. It's a good stopping point with this element for now. Your next task is to take the actions that you promised yourself. Revisit this section as you need, and evaluate how you're doing against your goals.

It's a great time to discuss your goals, plans, and learnings with friends and family. Here are journal pages where you can write about anything that comes to mind regarding this topic. We'll see you in the next section!

Action Steps - Here's What to Do Now:

You've now spent some time thinking about and working on some of the most important questions of your future. Well done! You're officially much wiser and much better than when you started!

I hope these simple exercises have created a way of thinking, and developed new skills that will help you create a vibrant life in the years ahead.

No one knows how life will unfold, but we all should have some sort of plan for it, and if you've worked through any of the elements in this workbook, you'll have a plan. Of course, life will most definitely change it. As boxer Mike Tyson once famously said: "Everybody has a plan until they get punched in the face".

For that reason, revisit this workbook from time to time – the frequency depends on how fast life changes occur. On those occasions, revisit these elements and work through your most important questions again.

One more thing – making the changes that you've identified in this book depends a lot on your mindset and attitude going forward. A small change in your mindset, beliefs and interests can improve your life. Change your mind to change your world.

It may be useful to take a look at this mindset checklist to include in your new journey:

Setting The Mindset Checklist

- Start by changing the way you talk to yourself because thoughts create reality and either help you progress or hold you back from your dreams.
- Change the way you talk to other people - maintain a positive attitude.
- Think and talk more about the things going well in your life than your problems.
- Create a mindset of abundance instead of a mindset of fear and negativity. ^
- Pick small goals for yourself and determine the mindset that can help you achieve these goals.
- Trick your brain into adopting a new thinking style and reinforcing it with your actions.
- Read more about people you admire and use learnings to adapt and improve your life.
- Surround yourself with positive people that can boost your energy
- Work on creating new and better habits that can help you achieve a positive change in life Learn to step out of your comfort zone to make needed changes.
- Find yourself people who can encourage you and who believe in your potential

Now here's a checklist summary of suggested next steps.

Next Steps Checklist

Quick Review

- ☐ Quickly page back through your notes, goals, and actions
- ☐ Note which ones have the most meaning for you

Take action

- ☐ Take action each day on your goals
- ☐ Revisit sections of this guide every few months and journal about your learnings
- ☐ Make adjustments to your goals as needed

Expand your knowledge

- ☐ Create a reading list of books you'll enjoy related to the most important elements
- ☐ Create a "watch list" of films and video that you'll enjoy related to these elements

Other Resources

- ☐ Make a list of friends, family members, and others you trust to discuss your progress
- ☐ 60Plus Living YouTube Channel
- ☐ Social Security: www.ssa.gov

About The Author

Greg is the author of other books available on Amazon, including: *"Own Your Reputation – A Guide To An Online Reputation That Attracts Customers, Clients, Patients, And Followers"*. And *"Cruise Like The Pros - A Beginner's Guide To A Revitalizing Getaway Cruise For Vacation Or Business"*.

In addition to his business interests, Greg has an interest in helping people to create a meaningful life as they age. *Wiser & Better!* is just one of the resources that serves this mission.

Greg began his business career as an engineer and progressed through senior management roles. He held corporate leadership positions for over 20 years, including Director of Engineering at Procter & Gamble, and Chief Innovation Officer with the Maytag Corporation.

Today, he runs the B2B Resource Team LLC, (formerly Peak Performance Solutions), a marketing and advertising agency whose mission it is to bring effective tools, methods and consulting to local businesses to improve their online presence.

The B2B Resource Team's primary services are in reputation management, digital ad campaign management, business copywriting, consulting and marketing strategies, and social media projects. You can learn more at www.b2bresourceteam.com.

Greg's client list reflects a broad range of experience and capabilities. He has served large and small clients and nonprofits in the consumer products, sports, pet services, real estate, health care, senior care, engineering, and government sectors.